INTEGRITY

INTEGRITY

VOLUME 1
The First Year
October–December 1946

CAROL JACKSON & ED WILLOCK, *EDITORS*

Foreword by Fr. James H. Doran

First Published by
Integrity Publishing Co., New York, 1946
Edited by Edward F. Willock and Carol Jackson
2019 © by Arouca Press
Foreword © Fr. James H. Doran 2019

All rights reserved:
No part of this book may be reproduced or transmitted,
in any form or by any means, without permission

ISBN 978-1-9994729-6-2

Arouca Press
PO Box 55003
Bridgeport PO
Waterloo, ON N2J3G0
Canada
www.aroucapress.com
Send inquiries to info@aroucapress.com

Book and cover design
by Michael Schrauzer

CONTENTS

Editor's Note vii
Foreword, *Fr. James H. Doran* ix

OCTOBER 1946 1

Editorial. 3
A Letter to an Editor about Our Lady,
   Herbert Thomas Schwartz. 9
Meditation in Mid-Manhattan, *Arthur Sheehan* 17
The Frustration of the Incarnation,
   Peter Michaels 21
Are You Ashamed of the Gospel?,
   Paul Hanly Furfey 37
The Perfect State, *Stanley Vishnewski*. 45
The Cross and The Dollar, *Ed Willock* 53
Book Reviews 67

NOVEMBER 1946 71

Editorial. 73
There is a Solution, *Paul McGuire* 77
Catholic Action in Canada, *Jim Shaw* 83
The Catholic Worker, *Dorothy Day*. 97
Apostles In Prison, *Donald L. Hessler* 107
The Leaven, *Peter Michaels* 121
The Workers' Apostolate, *John Fitzsimons*. 139
Book Reviews 147

DECEMBER 1946 153

Editorial. 155
The Captive, *John R. McCarthy*. 159
Integrity Incarnate, *James M. Egan, O.P.* 171
Celebration, *Jim Shaw* 183
In Bethlehem, *Jim Shaw* 184
Case 13,013, *Paul Hanly Furfey*. 189
The Gift Is Ours, *Ed Willock* 197
The Church Year Consecrating the March of Time,
  Jules A. Keating. 209
Book Reviews 215

APPENDIX: Prospectus 221

Editor's Note

THIS IS THE FIRST VOLUME OF A multi-volume project to republish all of the *Integrity* issues published from 1946 to 1956. The original editors were Carol Jackson Robinson (1911–2002) and Edward Willock (1916–1960). Dorothy Dohen (1924–1984) succeeded them as editor in 1952. All artwork by Ed Willock.

We wish to acknowledge the work of *The Angelus Press* for first re-introducing *Integrity* to the general public. Our work differs in so far as we wish to re-introduce the *entire* publication to the general public since these issues are relatively difficult to find. We also hope to spur a debate among informed Catholics to think about the issue of the integration of daily life and Faith in the modern world. Such ideas we believe are as important as they were when *Integrity* first attempted to analyze this issue over 70 years ago.

Foreword

IT CAN BE SUPPOSED THAT CAROL ROBINson had to have led an interesting life. Not interesting because torments, or wars, or trials had invaded her years, but because she had waged battles of the mind and navigated modernity over the surging waves of an unstable world. Grace, thought, and consideration had led her to the Catholic Faith, and grace and mind clearly filled her days throughout her adult life. She wished to be in the advance-guard of the Catholic battle against deception and the constant creep of infidelity that was filling and obscuring the modern world.

Although in 1990 I had already played a part in editing and publishing some of her writings from *Integrity* magazine, it had all been done through correspondence. She sent me a signed copy of that book once it had been published, but I had not met her. I first met Carol Robinson in the late 1990s, at which point she was well into her eighties. (She died in 2002.) Traveling a winding road through wooded land, another and I visited her in her colonial house, venerable in its age and itself filled with history. At that point in her life the wear and tear of age had touched her, as it does most all of us, and she was, as one says, "in her dotage," but two extraordinary things stood out in what was otherwise a simple visit to an elderly lady.

The first was how remarkable the setting. Here was a woman who had led an exceptionally vibrant and intellectual life often among the forefront of Catholic thought in America, and she inhabited a beautiful example of Connecticut colonial history: a twentieth-century Catholic convert dwelling in what was in effect a relic of the founding years of that Calvinist historical experiment that became the United States. The central part of the house was a chimney and the rooms radiated out from it. In a smallish room that had been clearly intended as a parlor it seemed evident that Mrs. Robinson prayed. There were devotional booklets beside a chair and funerary memorial cards had been attached to the wall opposite that chair. In many a pious person's prayer books these cards of *memento mori* fill the pages, warp the covers and flutter out as often as the book is opened. They are souvenirs of long lives filled with love and friendship. In this Connecticut house it seemed that most of these were not in books — although surely there were many unseen stuffed in pages elsewhere — but were attached to the wall surrounding the ancient fireplace and its mantle. Up and down the wall they went, over the mantle, farther up the wall, and, if memory serves me, down both sides of the fireplace. It was impressive. Striking not only because there were so many, but because almost all of them seemed to be mementoes of priests and bishops that Carol Robinson had known throughout her long and fruitful life. With all these before me, I was — a young priest just finishing my first decade of priesthood — profoundly touched at how "ecclesiastical" had been the woman in the kitchen. It was moving to witness just how momentous a life can be if one chooses to use one's God-given talents to the full.

The second memorable thing that afternoon took place toward the end of the visit. As I have said, the visit was similar to many I had made to other elderly people: small talk, chit-chat and superficial niceties. All was pleasant and expressive of true charity, but nothing earthshattering. On that autumn day, however, after we had spent a good hour or two visiting in the usual manner, it was as if a light had been turned on. In a totally unexpected way, from one moment to the next, there was a transformation that came over Mrs. Robinson and her conversation ignited. This may seem a bit of an exaggeration to say, but in an instant we went from chatting about weather and cookies to discussing religion, philosophy, and theology. It was as beautiful as it was startling in its transformation. For the next forty minutes or so we reveled in the world of Saint Thomas Aquinas, discussing the metaphysics of unbelief and the clouded thinking of modernity. If I had not already been convinced of the intellectual prowess of this woman through her writings that conversation, in that moment and on that day, would have done so. It is without exaggeration that I write that I have rarely ever had such a dazzling, thoughtful, and Catholic conversation with anyone: layman, priest or bishop (I've never conversed with a pope). It was edifying, but also touching and beautiful as, sadly, it dissipated as quickly as it had occurred. She lapsed back into her dotage and we were left to finish the visit with the accustomed politeness; and so we left.

About thirty years ago I was first introduced to *Integrity*, which would place that moment just over forty years from when the articles were first written. Now, in our convulsed and convulsing world seventy years is practically an eon, a world ago and a different age, indeed, it is painful at times to read the earnest thoughts of these writers. It was perhaps, with hindsight, a mercy of God that they could not know where we would be in less than a century. They lamented the loss of the Christian vision that had been fading away since the days of their grandparents, and which increased frighteningly during their own days following the Second World War. As young Catholic believers with an integral vision and acuity of mind, they had hoped that the hemorrhaging could be stopped. Reading these articles at times can be heartbreaking.

Now here we are, at the beginning of the third millennium of Christianity, among the ruins of the world they had hoped to rebuild in their day. What had received a severe body blow and had shown cracks in structural soundness in their times now smolders around us. The so-called "western world" is not healthy and its condition appears at moments to surely be terminal. So why reprint these articles with their thoughts, considerations, and proposed remedies? Do we romanticize earlier enthusiasts?

Surely not.

Treasures have been laid up for us. As we well know, God's Providence leads His Church all along the way, and especially from the mid-nineteenth to the mid-twentieth centuries were we given splendid magisterial statements and encyclicals on the Catholic social vision. The principles of social organization, economic thought, and political liberty were laid out brilliantly especially during the pontificates of Popes Gregory XVI, Pius IX, Leo XIII, Saint Pius X, Benedict XV, Pius XI and Pius XII. These teachings were true gifts to the world. As a Church, we have been prepared for this present moment. Those authoritative teachings laid out how faith and the Gospel should influence and mold the familial, social, public, and economic life of individuals, peoples, and nations. The principles remain perennially true and are rich ore from which enlightened minds, and hearts filled with charity, can still mine riches for this generation and for those to come. We need only apply ourselves to the task. All things may not be accomplishable in our historic moment, but, as ever, a true and complete vision is necessary to be mature in the tradition, patrimony, heritage, and orthodoxy of the one, apostolic, and holy Catholic Church.

Full. Complete. True. Whole. Catholic.

To every man, woman and child present in the world healing and restoration have been offered. Everyone has been redeemed by the Holy One's entrance into creation and human history, elevated by His glorification — ultimately bringing all into His majesty; but the actualization of this re-integration depends on each one's response to the divine invitation. Do we see creation as a vast domain for potential healing? Would we place ourselves among "the healthy" and quarantine by separation those for whom God means very little? Or, rather, would we be urged on by the example of the Risen One to extend the remedy of grace and favor to all? For our part, the restorative effects of grace result only from vision and free choice. Are we set to explain, confront, and clarify — or are we content to hide from strife, or flee from a world estranged from God?

In his first letter to the Ephesians, Saint Paul lays out the radical vision of cosmic restoration: all things are to be "re-capitulated" in the glorified God-Man, the Messiah, the One Who had been promised over the centuries through the Covenant established on Mount Sinai. The Holy One, the Son of the Most-High, drew His flesh, in time, from the ever-stainless womb of Mary of Nazareth and in so doing proposed to bring all creation, and all that man invents, into His final glory.[1] We now live in the "last days," which

---

1 "It is in the hope of Life that we are nourished by Thy Body and Blood; in the hope of victory that we fight; and in the hope of being greeted by Thee that we go out to meet Thee. Throughout our lives we hope, and all our hope is in Thee. Without Thee is neither hope nor life. Thou art the Hope and the One for Whom we hope, the means and the Goal, the First

means that all has been accomplished in Christ. In free collaboration, it remains for us to freely work out salvation's effects in time. This is the doctrine of Christ as "King." Not something to be accomplished in the future, at the *eschaton*: the Kingdom has been present among us from the days of John the Baptist, the Precursor.[2] Our responsibility is today.

Saint Isaac of Nineveh in his fifty-second homily described the three degrees of knowledge to be had in Christianity. The first degree is grounded in the "love of body." It is confined to what the senses can measure, quantify and analyze. The first degree of knowledge then is materialistic in its approach and locked into a downward gaze of existence. This is the philosophical starting point of today's "scientism" which diminishes so much of modern discourse. Saint Isaac states that this type of knowledge, relying only on the senses, is never free of uncertainty or fear. The second degree of knowledge is that originating in "the love of soul," which in faith and prayer initiates the purification of the spirit so that illumined by the faith it can perceive beyond mere sense knowledge. However, it is with the third degree of knowledge that we are most concerned here. This is "revelation," the unveiling that takes place as the Spirit of the Hidden One leads the purified mind and heart into the Mysteries that are inexpressible in words.

To any given individual it will be impossible to communicate the ineffable, to alone express what transcends human

---

and the Last. Divinity is enclosed in Thee and Thou dost renew all things in heaven and on earth, for all that is in heaven and on earth is through Thee and for Thee.... as we remember Thy Resurrection, we beseech Thee, O Lord, to realize one day in us the hope of new life that Thy Resurrection has given to us, and we will praise Thee, with Thy Father, and Thy Holy Spirit, now and forever." Sedro, *Safro*, Fifth Sunday of the Resurrection.

2 St. Luke 16:16, St. Matthew 11:12

experience, but to the whole Church, ancient and radiant in Tradition this is not the case. It is not so much that we quantify and measure the opinions expressed, but through the course of the apostolic centuries the holy statements of the saints have etched out a reliable communication (as humanly possible as this might be). The Fathers and the saints — within the *sensus fidei*, and from out of the "consciousness" of the Church of Christ — communicated as well as each could do in the circumstances of their times, using the fragility of human language. The expressions are of course locked in their historical context, but the Object expressed transcends any time. This is the basis of the Christian Tradition and Patrimony: what had been received was passed on. Tradition is transmitted revelation. After grace and faith, hope and charity, it is our greatest treasure. In the Syriac East, we refer to the *fenquitho* in which these things are held. The *fenquitho* was a box in which the family heirlooms and jewelry were kept and passed on from generation to generation. This is a perfect expression of our heritage as Catholics.

In each of our lives we slam into many things that are not understandable, which is why the elevated knowledge that our faith engenders brings peace and wisdom when we discover the greater certainty and deeper vision found in Christian tradition. This is our patrimony. Tradition belongs to no one and to every one of the baptized simultaneously — it depends on no one and is, as a whole, an expression of the Divine Logos in time. We find in it trustworthy guides in those things which are beyond our individual grasp. It contains a wisdom of a sacred family heritage and is not the separate possession of any. Where Saint Isaac's third degree of knowledge is manifest, the sensual first degree must give way and let loose its presumed certainty. Without recognizing the pre-eminence of this patrimony as a whole (in faith, charity, and hope) there is no Christianity.

Follow in the footsteps of the Fathers and our path is assured.

Tradition and our sacred patrimony do express the mind and the will of the Hidden Savior, but we must not lose sight that their fullness encompasses all the sacred guides East and West (and, we must add, the "fully" East): Latin, Hellenic, Coptic, and Syriac. All too often some speak of the Church as composed of "east and west" meaning only Constantinople and Rome, and they drop any real reference to the rest of the Apostolic Church. This is a deficient approach. At the end of the first century, the Petrine and Patriarchal Churches were Antioch, Rome, and Alexandria—centuries before Constantinople even existed, let alone being recognized as patriarchal. This malformed concept of Christianity is tragic in its misunderstanding and bespeaks an insufficient Catholic vision, although this insufficiency is both an ancient and understandable one.

During the decisive years of the Church's liberation and social formation in the fourth century, Rome extended into the western part of Mesopotamia, and even then only periodically, depending on battles won against the Persian Empire. That part of the Great Church which developed in the eastern region of Syria, and especially in Mesopotamia and further east into what is now Iran was left outside any real awareness of the Romans. In Eusebius' *Ecclesiastical History* there is almost nothing stated about the Church as she was outside the Empire. The *Oikoumene* was the Roman Empire, and this thought has colored the Byzantine and Roman understandings to this day. For this reason, so much of Christian Church history remains Euro-centric.

This is why, when a Latin Catholic speaks about "the east" today she usually means "Byzantine," but Constantinople is still eastern *European* for the most part. When a Byzantine Christian speaks of the East, he often may refer to the Syriac Church, but this means to its writers as adopted and Hellenized by Constantinople. Saint Ephraim "the Syrian" in his monastic Greek form shares little resemblance to the *malphono* of Nisibis, the Harp of the Spirit of *Urhoy*. The Church of Constantinople may be a daughter of Antioch, but she remains a Hellenic and European daughter.[3]

Moreover, since the Middle Ages the Latin West has been somewhat myopic in its view of the apostolic patrimony and has too readily locked "tradition" into only what the Church of Rome has done, along with a smattering of ancient Greeks at times. Communion with the Apostolic See guarantees our orthodoxy in the faith, but that is not surety that we live the full richness of that faith without our brothers and sisters in eastern Europe and the Middle East. There is a rich oriental heritage that is only now coming to be known by the European Church. Although wonderful, this is also tragic. It is wonderful because the *fenquitho* of the East is filled, waiting to be opened by the Hellenic and Latin western traditions. At the same time, it is tragic as this often has been the result of easterners fleeing their homelands with these treasures under their arms and in their baggage as it were. It repeats to some extent the events enriching Italy in the fifteenth century when Byzantine scholars fled the Turkish invasion and fall of Constantinople. We become aware of our eastern brothers as Christianity disappears from its cradle. As a

---

3   In their formation, the Maronites have been a juncture between the "western Syriac" and "eastern Syriac," and, at least since the Crusades, a bridge between "east" and "west" as in "Middle Eastern" and "European."

result of this flight, the rich Syriac traditions and churches now traverse the continents. We call this "the Expansion."

There is one Christian and Catholic Faith, but diverse angles. We should enrich our thought for a more strategic and apostolic future.

In the Syriac tradition of Christianity — those churches of Jerusalem and Antioch which originated among the first converts from ancient Israel — from out of the lands of Mesopotamia and ancient Syria, the perspective of redemption can be contrasted to the commonly held western view. While Constantinople and Rome have stressed the entrance of the Eternal God into time through the Incarnation, the Churches of the East placed greater prominence on the elevation of humanity to the Good One, stressing the *homo assumptus* in the Incarnation. All orthodox Christianity recognizes the grace of God as both reparative and elevating, but the transformation through elevation is given the greater importance in the less juridically minded east. This is sometimes termed as *a return to Paradise*, not as a utopian vision, but as a return to a state originally intended by the Creator, when the human race existed in intimacy with the Hidden Father and when God "walked in the Garden." Hence, in its Aramaic liturgical poetry, in the fullness of time the Messenger sent to Nazareth is portrayed as bearing "a letter" from the Hidden Father to the Virgin of Nazareth. This Communication cannot be spoken by creation, but which, in her hearing and through her "fiat," was engraved within the flesh of the untarnished and all-spotless Virgin, the Daughter of David. Thus, having been "written by her pen,"[4] the Mystery hidden from before the foundation of the world was finally made known

---

4 Fenqitho, *Proemion* from the Feast of Our Lady of the Seeds, May 15th.

to mankind. She is the New Garden which brought forth the New Tree of Life to the world, and became as it were the inscription and the exordium of the Divine Kingdom restored. Now this is a concrete view of redemption.

The Man born to *Maryam* of Nazareth is the New Adam and the One Who has come not to take us "somewhere" — even if it be "heaven" — but One Who is the Hidden Word in Whose Incarnate Image (according to the ancient Fathers) mankind was first formed. Note well that in this view humanity was not created according to some philosophical or ethereal image of an unknown "eternal Intellect and Will" but according to the eternally known Messiah, God-made-Flesh. *Adom* was created in the image of Christ. In this Image, flesh was first drawn from the soil of Paradise and life was breathed into it. In the Annunciation that eternal Reality Itself entered time so that humanity might be raised back up to the true measure according to which it had been first created.

Why this long digression into the Orient?

This Syriac "concreteness" should remind us that our Catholic Faith is not merely a thing for "saving souls," and perhaps this oriental vision might even inspire us to act in accord with the truth that revelation is meant to radiate outward from the Christ, touching each person and transforming his or her milieu in the New Creation.[5] All that is human

---

5 "O Messiah, in the light of this morning, let Thy Resurrection shine upon us. Through Thy Resurrection Thou hast renewed heaven and earth, made man a new creature, and sent the Breath of Thy Hope into the world. Bless this morning with the blessings of the morning of Thy Resurrection, so that we may accomplish all works of *shlom* and piety. May we be worthy of the Morning of Thy Kingdom, where the sun never sets, and we will glorify and praise Thee, forever. Amen." Opening Oration, *Safro*, Thursday of the Resurrection.

must be encompassed by grace. Evil is averted, sin is healed, and death is transformed into life. Suffering and pain acquire purpose and become redemptive. This is all true for both our individual and social lives. We must be transformed by grace in a corporate manner as well as in an individual one.

This digression is also meant as a reminder in our postmodern western world that we have far too easily succumbed to the lethal dissociation of religion from life. We are not Neo-Platonists, we are Catholics. We do not seek some escape to a spiritual realm of bliss, but to join with the Messiah, the Word Incarnate, as He works the remedial redemption of the cosmos. Cosmos? Absolutely, a new heaven and a new earth in which justice dwells.[6]

Grace, redemption, spiritual practice, and holiness are habitually dissociated from our workaday lives. This is seductive as selfishness flatters within, and grace burns away dross. It is easier to embrace the darkness, because cloaked by it disorder is not seen. As one will find written herein, the light of hell flatters and leads to illusion (delusion), but the brilliant light of faith (often) blinds in an experience of darkness. Lived over the years, this paradox becomes "tangible." We must re-integrate a complete vision of the faith into every detail of our lives as they are actually lived in this world. *Integrity*.

All too often today, the Catholic Faith, indeed religion in general, has become a kind of disembodied fairy-tale that we hope will give us nice feelings here below and later supply us with a ticket to some "happy place" after death. Seen this way, it *is* a "crutch" to be used when needed, if ever, good for individuals, perhaps, but which has nothing to do with the "real world" in which we "really" live. It is no wonder

6 II Peter 3:13

that millennials have generally dropped it all *en masse*. Many Catholics (most?) have forgotten the ancient axiom that Christianity is a life to be lived and a "way" that is to be followed. It is not just a story; it is an identity: an identification with the Living One on Golgotha, and with the Risen One as origin of the New Creation.

The famous English convert Douglas Hyde communicated as much in the years following his entrance into the Church. He told us not to be afraid to demand much from believers — especially the young — as Our Lord Himself had done in the Gospel. As a recruiter for the Communist Party he knew well that identity, example of sacrifice, and dedication were the only things that would attract others to "a cause." We have forgotten this psychological truth as we bent over backward for the last century and a half to make the Catholic Faith "easy." Demand little and expect even less, became the motto. In truth, this seems to have been the axiom for many over these last generations, both of the priests and of the parents of the baptized. "Make it too hard and they will all leave," was the expressed thought (who knows what they actually believed) and this vacuous mantra continues to be repeated even today.[7] This was an example of the deceptive "light" of hell, and death has been the result.

Religion in the modern world has been reduced to emotion and mere sentiment, feelings. If it is lived by some, it has been all too often reduced to a form of innocuous

---

7   Bizarre, truly, as those who repeat this absurdity now stand in empty churches and among the rubble of faith. They weep over their now unbaptized grandchildren. *We return to a wounded and fallen world through the agency of inept Christians.* One would think that the clear result of this century-long experiment would have proven the fallaciousness of the premise.

humanitarianism, reducing the Gospel to the natural law and questions of natural justice.[8] The first example is a purely individual affair of "whatever" — thus safely ignored with little consideration — and the latter has seemed inoffensive enough to modern eyes.

Among many, where the faith is still believed and cherished, there has been an almost obsessive pursuit of "common ground" among "men of good will," and while this is all good in itself, this seeking of common ground has risked, does risk, undermining the apostolate of proclaiming the Gospel of the Risen One, which is not based on "common agreement" but on the eruption of grace and redemption in the midst of a fallen world. "Comfortable" has never been a description of the apostolic endeavor. While divine grace always proposes to illumine, heal, and elevate, it is not always pleasant in the recipient. Consensus has never been an apostolic approach. It smacks of naturalism and the vague sentiment that somehow "good" people are already "there."[9]

Grace by definition, certainly initial grace, cannot be merited, so an approach of building up natural goodness as if it were somehow redemptive or a better basis for the

---

8 Even this has not been done well as the prohibitions of abortion and artificial "birth control" are classic examples of the natural law. So far have modern men veered off from the path of right reason, these "teachings" are now considered "Catholic" doctrine as if only the Catholic Church somehow "made them up."

9 "We all go 'to heaven'," it is stated *ad naseam*, as if the inevitable act of dying changed a person from what he had been two days before. We die the way we have lived. Hence there is a particular judgement at the moment of death. Grace has not been given to the world to "clean up" whatever human beings decide to do with their lives. It is the manifestation of the Good One, the basis of His "kingdom," so that man might enter definitively into His Unique Existence transformed and godlike. "Nice" is not the quintessential attribute of redemption.

life of grace verges on heresy, and yet it is the basic principle of action for so many. Grace, we must never forget, bears the imprint of both Golgotha and the Resurrection. Surely, many of the temple priests at the time of the Messiah were "decent men," or do we think that the crowds shouting for Our Lord's crucifixion were all inveterately evil and that people of today are "better"? If so, better in what way? Better because they have indoor plumbing or better social media? We deceive ourselves so easily; darksome in itself, hell is luminous to the blind. Heaven is not pulled down to earth by men, it is men that are raised up to the Hidden Light. Rather than making excuses for contemporary mediocrity, the Hidden God of all consolation demands from us the opening of hearts to an unseen and unforeseeable transformation of future possibilities that only He can achieve through grace. This has ever been the case.

Well, I think we can all agree that this contemporary mindset, along with its modern apostolic program of ease, has achieved its goal, it has been "a success": comfortably, generations now have wandered away from redemption, the spirit of discipleship and sacrifice has evaporated, and little remains of substance today in many churches. The scandal has been enormous. But take courage, you have before you the example of numerous writers who took up this challenge before us.

Among these articles, and in the volumes to follow, you will find many considerations and reminders of the foundation which must be laid ever new. Each generation is apostolic in that we receive the faith transmitted from the Apostles, and by the certainty that we must live that same faith as the Apostles once did themselves. As with philosophy, each generation must enter, perceive, assimilate, and incarnate the faith. The material sciences can build on the research of others without duplicating previous experiments, but the faith can only advance by being lived. It is renewed in each generation in that it is incarnated once again within the Body of Christ, the Church, and, indeed, in each faithful man and woman who is so illuminated, and then it is transmitted as a living reality to those who follow. By grace and love, we are links in a chain that stretches from *Adom* to the *Parousia*.

Many pagans know the "Jesus story," but that does not bring them any closer to the healing grace of redemption. So it is with many Catholics who still call themselves by that name: they know the "Jesus story," but it has almost nothing to do with the way they live their "real" lives. Grace burns, and "narrow is the gate" that leads to Life.[10] We must recover the sense of conviction, dedication, devotion, and discipleship that has *always* raised up martyrs; and in the meantime, before that witness of death, others seeing that redeeming light of the New Creation in life and action, will be drawn to its beauty with conviction. This is how the Good Tidings of the New Creation have always been transmitted — from the morning of the Resurrection — and it is how they will continue to do so until the Manifestation of Our Lord on the Last Day.

For these reasons, and following the ancient Catholic path, the writers of these articles and volumes of *Integrity* have rendered a great service by reminding one and all that Christianity must be lived or else it is nothing. All that is properly human enters its sweeping view: individual virtue, of course, but also social life, family, child rearing, education, political governance, economic decisions, etc. The New Adam came to elevate all that is human in its integrity and

---

10 St. Matthew 7:14

return it to its original Image. Catholicism touches all the details of human existence, and only those things which cannot be transformed and elevated by grace are such by their intrinsic disorder. These latter particulars are unworthy of the children of God, the disciples of Word Incarnate, and, as Saint Paul wrote, should not even be mentioned among us.[11] So it is that Catholicism, when fully alive, is "integral Catholicism," and by such we must confront the predicament of our age.

The light of the Gospel is a vision of fullness within the ancient and ever true tradition of the Church, both as the Sacred Deposit[12] and as the full patrimony bequeathed to us within the apostolic Churches. Sadly, among some, in the modern defense of orthodoxy and integral Catholicism, the combat for doctrinal fidelity can become embittered. There can be a temptation to descend into a too human understanding of what is called "doctrinal purity" that is emotionally Cathar, violent in feeling and bitter in its exclusive sentiment. In this, the devil wins twice over. We must strive, we must combat, and we must wage battle in a fully committed devotion to the life-giving and luminous Cross, but our war is not against other men, but with the powers and principalities of this world of darkness.[13] The success of the devil is that he has made many strident in their attempted defense, and unappealing in their call to Catholic Truth. *Bitter zeal* this has always been called. This embittered battle may become, emotionally and mentally at least, schism as it "severs" and "cuts away" in its struggle to preserve. The proclamation of the Gospel must be done "in season and

---

11 Ephesians 5:3
12 St. Jude 1:3
13 Ephesians 6:12

without" but it must be done with "all patience and teaching,"[14] even with face hardened against all obstacles — three cheers for Saint Athanasius the Great — but also by conquering in the footsteps of the Sacred Heart and by imitating the Shepherd brought up again from the dead.[15] It is ultimately the martyrs who have been the most eloquent — and successful — defenders of truth. Are we prepared to die for it, or are we just looking to win an argument?

The clarity of full, faithful, and true *integrism* allows us to appreciate the historical fact that in practice every heresy has erupted throughout the ages by absolutizing a truth or some element of doctrine. As Luther focused obsessively on the detail of the gratuitousness of redemption, so in the end he distorted and mutilated the proper understanding of salvation, the virtue of faith, and human free-will. His thought emptied the Divine and Sacramental Mysteries of any intrinsic reality. These are noteworthy consequences from an exaggeration of one element of truth. Unavoidably becoming lopsided, this approach inevitably topples into error. Without the integrity of the Catholic faith as lived in its balanced fullness, individualistic willfulness engenders a lack of wholeness, a defect of integrity, and (pushed to its sad logic) false and heretical teaching. Adherence to personal opinion becomes adamant and breaks out as heresy; and heresy always spawns schism. Charity is violated in the name of the chosen "truth," and supernatural faith is offended.

On the contrary, let those who read these pages pursue with utmost strength through healing grace to the fullness of true integral Catholicism: practiced, lived and nurtured

---

14   II Timothy 4:2
15   Hebrews 13:20

in the full patrimony of Apostolic Tradition. We must not obsess over aspects of the Catholic Faith, but seek a full equilibrium in understanding it. This requires ongoing catechesis and the dissatisfaction with any present practice of the Faith we have acquired. There is always a next step to take on the path of the Gospel. We know there is always a greater depth to enter when it comes to the Faith. East, West, and all the Fathers must be the sources from which we draw the living-waters of Christ the King. We must be especially cautious in our defense of the Faith in the present disarray of the world so that we do not inadvertently follow the path of Luther. The zeal would be bitter, the charity cold, and the end result untruthful in its distortion. The Faith is more than an argument to be won, and the best testimony to truth is a radiantly peaceful life of witness. This must begin in our personal — and daily — conversion to the Unclouded Bright One, the Good One Who elevates those who respond to His gracious invitation. In conversion, we transform the mind and renew our attitudes as we seek to unify our public and private lives, that our recreation, work, "business," and tech all be illuminated by the same light of the Word Incarnate that we claim to know from our catechism.

Collaboration with the Kingdom as proclaimed by the Messiah requires the "violence" of the strong,[16] and this we ask to be fulfilled each day in the *Pater Noster*. It must be freely and generously given. This effort may often enough result in failure according to the judgement of the world, but faithful cooperation with the Word Incarnate is never a failure regardless of the tangible effects. Failures remind us that we are not in charge, and that the smallness of humility

---

16 St. Matthew 11:12

that it engenders grounds us in truth and justice, generally better than does success. One may be called to live in obscurity, but the radiance of prayer and the strength of fasting are omnipresent. The faithful, prayerful, and contemplative soul in the supernatural order is much like a tree on the earth: it clears out the impurities of the atmosphere. As trees cleanse the carbon dioxide from the air, so the faithful and prayerful purify the atmosphere of this fallen world. Unseen, but efficacious all the same. These individuals may never be known in this world; they may never win an argument or celebrate a victory "for truth," but all shall be manifested on the Day of the Lord, "shouted from the housetops."[17] Meanwhile, even if called to littleness in our time, we will have contributed to the integral vision of the faith that brings life to the world. As stated succinctly in the magazine's introduction so many years ago, "integrity is at the opposite pole from expediency." While all are needed, the hidden ascetic and the faithful hermit do more for the world than the most brilliant apologist, and the martyr is the perfect ascetic accomplishing the most. Humility. Seeking the Mind of Christ,[18] we are less tempted to think ourselves to be "something" and thus fall into illusion.

Death of the mind necessarily leads to death of the soul and spirit. While many unlearned people may attain holiness, ignorance is not a virtue, rather it is often an obstacle to grace as it befuddles the mind. This must be overcome by the light of the faith. Ignorance is not a source of strength leading one to the light of the Kingdom, no matter how holy God may judge an individually ignorant man. What

---

17 St. Matthew 10:26–27
18 Philippians 2

one will find in these pages is an attempt "to make a new synthesis of Religion and Life," an integration of the natural and supernatural orders, and a restoration of the harmony once experienced at the beginning of our race but now raised up in the New Creation. It is a view that is in complete accord with the centuries of saints and faithful that have gone before us, those who have handed down to us the light of the New Adam as embodied in His Church. Likewise, devotion requires us to seek an integration of spirit and praxis that is illuminated as one life, one elevation, and one *shlomoh/salus*/salvation bequeathed to us, a gift unveiled through the Hidden One's Radiance.

These articles and reprinted volumes are a treasure because they were written by older contemporaries wrestling with a world we recognize. By thought and pen, they fought the good fight within a world that is still very much our own — albeit more degenerate in these our days. Severe illness left untreated leads to death, and the last four centuries have witnessed a cancerous descent into madness. Think "mad cow disease" in the Christian West and we have rather good simile of the philosophical and religious condition of what was once Christendom. Nevertheless, the light of the Gospel is as ever brilliant for those who have eyes to see and ears to hear. God is as omnipotent today as He was on Golgotha.

As it was especially prophetic, I call attention to the article entitled, "The Frustration of the Incarnation." These last decades much energy has been spent in the pursuit of a fairy-tale-like "common ground" with non-Catholics. I say "fairy-tale," because so much of the work has been done without reference to revelation as found in the full patrimony of the Church. To discover a "common ground" of agreement necessitates ignoring many details of that patrimonial fullness. Now, it is an excellent thing to have cordial relations with those around us, the charity of Christ requires us to do so, but this modern quest has been so constant that even now most Catholics have little idea, if any, of the Church's profound and coherent vision in Christ. Not only have non-Catholics not been brought to the fullness of the Gospel, most Catholics, if they think at all on religious matters, diverge not at all from the general population which surrounds them. *Statistically*, modern Catholics contracept and abort their children on par with their non-Catholic neighbors, and the majority of Catholics seem to no longer believe in the Eucharistic Presence. For those Catholics who do try to be faithful, straining at least to move forward from among the commonality of their fellows, the topics of "abortion" and "contraception" have become presently thought to be quintessentially "Catholic" doctrines whereas they are in fact nothing more than the natural law — discernible by all who possess lucidity of mind and good-will to consider the works of nature. Noble truths, certainly, and necessary to propose and defend, but these are not perfect examples of the full light of revelation.

The salt has lost its savor; *insipid*, as a people we are no longer lights to the world or stars shining out among a perverse generation as Saint Paul once wrote.[19] Two generations have now practically been lost to the Church as the Faith has not been transmitted, and what little catechesis there has been, was swamped by the cacophony of superficial modernity. It is said, again statistically, that for every individual who enters the Catholic Church six previously baptized walk away from it. We will remain in a very sad state

---

19 Philippians 2:15

until a supernatural vision once again arises among those of us who are meant to be the disciples of the Word Incarnate. May all throw aside the false sentimentality in which we have floundered for much of a century, and mature from out of a childish view of the Faith. This can be accomplished by none other than ourselves who have already received the light of faith, and it will only come about through living, teaching, and catechizing the flock once again, and proclaiming the Gospel to those outside the Fold.

Mr. Barbas is to be congratulated for assembling once again for print these articles, poems, and essays — and even the cartoons (perhaps, *especially* the cartoons) — they contain clarity of thought more often than not, and lay out the principles of a Catholic vision that sees the healing grace of redemption as a whole. These authors clearly believed, as the Church has always done, that the salvation of the world is an integral whole: mind, spirit, soul, body, family, community, work, and culture. The Eternal One entered time to heal it, transformed nature as the New Adam, and set to restore the cycle of existence into transformed and sacred moments leading to the imperishable Kingdom. The Good One became man so that human beings individually and as a whole could be restored and elevated entirely in their being, relations, loves, sufferings, disappointments, hopes and labor. The Divine Word entered a wounded and off-kilter cosmos, so that the Divine Economy could be made manifest in Him and radiate out among all and therapeutically restore all things, healing all from the inside out. The luminous source of this consoling vision has always been found in the apostolic teachings and in the deposit of the faith possessed by the Church of Christ. The fundamental ideas of which these authors write — whether in the 1940s, or as read by us in 2019 — remain permanently true, because they reflect the permanence of the immutable Logos of the Hidden Light in the eternal Now.

It is a blessing that Carol Robinson, Ed Willock and the others were not only thinkers for the common man, but also writers. They thought about the hard questions challenging modern Christians and they did not hesitate to put forward answers with equally adamantine responses. As their considerations and writings are so often based on the perennial wisdom of the great Catholic thinkers, they remain useful to this day, clearing a trail for those of us who live in a less thoughtful world. For this we can be grateful. These writers were prescient in foreseeing the future world of Catholicism as already it had begun to dawn in the early twentieth century. Some of the circumstances and historical details of these articles are of course dated, but the thoughts laid out by the authors are well worth the time to read and *ponder*. Pray on them even.

Humanly speaking, our modern predilection for speed is a disaster in even the best settings as it makes us superficial, but in the realm of thought it is catastrophic. One now emotes and reacts, rarely is any discussed topic clarified or defined. This is a principal reason why modern social discourse is habitually held at the volume of a shriek or indignant scream. Superficiality makes for a morally shallow person, one who skitters about his life among his "stuff." Sadly, years ago, we passed through the looking-glass into the land of tweets. Superficiality is the death of thought; and when it becomes the predominant intellectual fault, or "default" mode as it would be said these days, we are doomed to questing the highly praised characteristic of Orwell's *1984*: to become "double-plus-good duck speakers." This, he wrote, was the highest achievement in Big Brother's world and the greatest accolade that could be bestowed on a "citizen," that is, to be one who could speak freely and rapidly — spitting out words — with (and this is the key) the smallest amount of engaged mental activity.

I leave you to answer whether or not we have already arrived in that place.

REV. FR. JAMES H. DORAN
Saint Joseph Antiochene Syriac Maronite Catholic Church
Waterville, Maine

New Sunday
April 28, 2019

INTEGRITY

:the first issue:

A Magazine about Catholic Lay Life Today.

October 1946
VOLUME 1, NUMBER 1

EDITORIAL

THIS IS THE FIRST ISSUE OF *INTEGRITY*. It is the first fruit of the labor and prayers of the staff and our writers, the first opportunity for our subscribers to test the confidence they have placed in us. We have promised much, as not a few people have reminded us. One priest writes:

> The Millenium is in view, and I am hereby sending my subscription to insure a seat in the front row. You see, I am young Father McFadden, and, after six years with Amalgamated Teacup, one very weary Vigilante.[1] Unlike your Father McFadden, I am delighted to admit that I don't know the answers; and my three dollars express the fond hope that you do.

Well, Father McFadden, here is the beginning of our answer.

In this first issue we are elaborating on the theme of our whole magazine, which is: WE MUST MAKE A NEW SYNTHESIS OF RELIGION AND LIFE. Possibly the Church has other tasks yet more urgent today, but this job is certainly high up on the agenda. It looks like the basic problem for

---

[1] The references are to our prospectus. [See Appendix. —Ed.]

us, who are lay people. Anyhow, we have chosen it as our special work to help solve it, and every issue will bear on the main thesis.

We wanted to say something about the Virgin Mary in the first issue, not just out of piety, but because ours promises to be the age of Mary, and it seems as though the return of mankind to God will be accomplished through Her instrumentality. This will sound like madness to those who hear it for the first time. Yet we feel that the degree to which Our Lady seems irrelevant to our present problems is the measure of our lack of Christian understanding. Why, at this late date, should there be agitation in the Church for a definition of the doctrine of the Assumption?* Why should Mary have appeared three times in the last century, and to children? A Catholicism which cannot integrate these facts into its world view must be off focus. Yet it is not an easy subject, nor one which readily appeals to our modern minds. We give first place in this issue to an explanation of why Mary is especially important today. The author, Herbert Schwartz, has been good enough to simplify it as much as possible. Humility rather than erudition is the key to understanding it.

The worship of the state is darkest folly. It is the pit into which all of us will be plunged if we don't think sharply, and Germany's sordid example will not necessarily save us. Remember the exaggerated Americanism recently displayed on the backs of telephone books and on billboards? It read something like this: "Neither Catholic, Jew, nor Protestant—but American." Nobody seemed

---

* The dogma of the Assumption was solemnly defined by Pope Pius XII on November 1, 1950 in the Apostolic constitution, *Munificentissimus Deus*. —Ed.

perturbed at the implication that it was more important to be an American than to be a Christian. Father Paul Hanly Furfey* (*Are You Ashamed of the Gospel?*) points out the danger of statism (as he calls the worship of the state) here in America. He represents it as the inadvertent outcome of the prevalent doctrine of liberalism, and warns Catholics that they, too, foster it by selective presentation of the Church's social doctrine.

In a lighter vein, Stanley Vishnewski pictures *The Perfect State* toward which our worship of the state is tending.

Integral Catholicism is already becoming a popular expression. It does not mean piety so much as wholeness. It means that what we profess to believe is consistent with the assumed principle by which we live out our daily lives. It suggests a consistency of theory and practice; a unity of public life and private morals; a reconciliation of commercial ethics and religious dogma, of individual conscience and statutory law. It means a cessation of the uneasy Sunday-lip-service-to-God-and-40-hours-a-week-with-time-and-one-half-for-overtime-devotion-to-Mammon by which so many of our lives are compromised. The relationship between "wholeness" and "holiness" is as direct as the derivation of the second word from the first. It becomes daily more difficult to lead holy lives in disregard of the contradictory nature

---

* Fr. Paul Hanly Furfey (1896–1992) was a trained sociologist who had a wide-ranging influence as a priest dedicated to social issues. He had a long career spending much of it at the Catholic University of America. In 1940, he proposed a *supernatural sociology* which would take cognizance of the data of revelation a position which was not without its opponents. His development with regards to sociology certainly developed throughout the years but as indicated in his contributions to *Integrity* and his personal letters to the editors (Carol Jackson and then Dorothy Dohen) he was in full support of the goals of this ambitious periodical. — Ed.

of the circumstances thereof.

The guiding policy of contemporary society is expediency. Don't act from high moral principles (it's impractical). Don't commit yourself either to thorough-going villainy (it isn't nice). Just compromise, adjust, submit, water down, and make the best of a bad situation (after all, we have to eat). Our expediency looks less and less like the "sane policy of realistic leaders" and more and more like the degrading opportunism of ignoble men.

Integrity is at the opposite pole from expediency. It is a quality which does not look first to the financial consideration involved, does not calculate its actions to please high worldly powers, or with an eye to the coming elections. It does not hold that the end justifies the means, but that we must do what is right, come what may. We hope to achieve it ourselves and in our magazine.

Our generation is in for a synthesis of doctrine and practice anyhow. The only question is whether doctrine is going to defer to practice or vice versa. We came perilously near, here in America to achieving a complete commercial synthesis, as Ed Willock points out in *The Cross and the Dollar*. Perhaps the past tense is ill-advised. Yet the materialistic synthesis does seem to be giving away to something rather worse.

It is easy to suggest a re-integration of religion and life, but where do you start? We thought a long time over this one before we decided on the root problem. We could see that the real synthesis did not lie on the natural or ethical level. We were sure it didn't lie just in the intensification of devotions, as though the movies would improve for having the MGM employees spend longer over their night prayers (if they say night prayers). We decided the root problem is that of the integration of the natural and supernatural orders, a thesis elaborated by Peter Michaels (Carol Jackson) in *The Frustration of the Incarnation*.

This, then, is our new magazine. We are grateful to our writers, and grateful to our subscribers. Because it is our child, we are pleased with it. Because it is just a child, we look forward to its growth and development.

THE STAFF

A LETTER TO AN EDITOR ABOUT OUR LADY

DEAR CAROL,

As I sat before the typewriter, wondering how to begin the little essay on Our Blessed Mother which I had promised you, I was struck by this evident fact, how easy it was to talk to you of Our Lady, and how embarrassing it was, somehow, to write about Her. Then I thought that this was all very much related to the point and purpose of my writing — because what had embarrassed me was the idea of being an author, instead of a collaborator with the Author, and with Mary Who is His first Collaborator. That was why, as soon as I found myself alone with the intention of writing about Mary, the thought filled me with dismay, as though I had been called upon to manifest Herbert Thomas Schwartz. And with that thought, any power I might have was gone. Thus thrown back on myself, I was all confusion and shame. But when I was talking with you, your love of Our Lady overcame my love of myself, so that together we could praise Her, drinking in the peace of self-forgetfulness in the rightful pride we could take in Mary, the Mother of God, and our Mother.

* * *

THAT IS WHY I AM WRITING IN THE FORM OF A letter, so that the memory of our love of Mary may overcome that impotence of self-love. And that, as I have said, has very much to do with the purpose of my writing. There are many ways we could begin, but in the end the same truth will emerge, so it isn't really too important. But this idea reoccurs again and again, and so I think it is the way She would like it expressed: the name of your magazine is *Integrity*, and the name of Our Lady as She has announced it for our times is *The Immaculate Conception*. Well I suspect that the name you have chosen is that very name of the Blessed Virgin, at least in principle. I could make my meaning clearer by defining integrity in a way very fashionable now, and which I am sure you would not accept, the "integrity" of Kierkegaard. Poor Kierkegaard was in love with purity which, as he well knew, was very intimately connected with integrity. But his idea of purity, and integrity, was what you can realize by your own activity. That is why he is a Protestant and a modern prophet. Because men since the Renaissance have been trying to realize the integrity which man can attain by his own unaided efforts. And because what we do by such effort must proceed from our own judgment, our culture of light, the culture of Lucifer, the "Light-bearer." But Mary, who is the Archenemy of Lucifer, pleads with Her children not to be misled because She is black. There are two integrities, therefore, the integrity which is light, the lure of God's first enemy who has transformed himself into an Angel of Light, and the integrity of darkness, the integrity of the Immaculate Conception.

All our difficulties in the order of doctrine arise from the failure to distinguish *Her darkness, which is light*, from the flattering *light of hell, which is darkness*. How do we fall into this error? By an undue love of light. But what makes this love undue, for assuredly it is our love of light that makes us hunger for that First of all light, and certainly, then, there is nothing wrong in our love of light as such? But what was excessive when Eve was seduced by the serpent? Her judgement, whereby she judged that the fruit was pleasant and good to eat, for in this she placed *the light of her judgment* before the *darkness of the Divine command* which forbade her to eat of the fruit. Observe, too, how quick Satan was to exploit this pride of judgment, telling Eve that she would not die by eating of this fruit, that, on the contrary, she and Adam would become as gods. But God had said they would surely die.

Eve was motivated by "integrity" in giving her assent to the devil's temptation: for, in that sense of integrity, a judgement is more perfect when it proceeds from principles which are evident to us. Under such circumstances, we are not divided, our intellect tending one way, our practical decisions another. But when we would live according to Faith we are torn between the two principles — until the merely human one (less than human through sin) dies.

I think that was what Mary intended to teach us when She declared Herself a handmaid of the Lord, that is, an instrument. As Aristotle called the hand the instrument of instruments because it fashions and employs all the others, so we should call Mary the Instrument of Instruments in the supernatural order. It is very instructive to compare the two terms, *instrument* and *principle*. Thus the musician performing is a *principle* of the music produced, because a principle is a beginning, that from which something proceeds, as the Father in the Blessed Trinity is the First of all principles. But the device, through which the music comes to us, the piano or violin, is not a principle, but an instrument merely, that *through* which the music is communicated. To adapt the metaphor, God is looking for a musical instrument which will be sensitive to His every nuance of desire: but we all want to be the musicians. (I think that the harp of David symbolized Our Lady, its seven strings the seven Gifts of the Holy Ghost.) The reason we are such poor musicians is that we have forgotten how to be instruments. Perhaps that sounds like a paradox, but we mean the same thing when we say that "he who cannot obey cannot command," and the industrialist father who insists that his son start from the very bottom in his factory, has grasped the same truth. To state it more directly, God wants us to be gods, and not merely His instruments, but we can only acquire that principality through the apprenticeship whereby we are perfected as His instruments.

OUR VOCATION, THEN, IS TO BE LIVING INSTRU-ments, as Christ our Lord was a living Instrument of the Father. But an instrument implies an instrument maker. If we are to be the instruments of God, we must be formed as that First Instrument was formed, in Mary, and not only in Mary, as a plant is formed in the earth, but *by* Her, as it is Her loving cooperation which brought God to us in the Incarnation. Mary, then, is the Artist Who, together with the Holy Ghost, must bring us, Her Children to the perfection of Christ, Her First-born. Our Lord did not say "Unless you are born again of the Holy Ghost," merely, but "Unless you are born again of *water* and the Holy Ghost." Why water? Was Christ Himself born of water and the Holy Ghost? He was born of Mary and the Holy Ghost. And as every Christian is baptized by water, he is a child of Mary. Mary is His Mother, not as a figure of speech, but in the literal sense of the term, as a mother is a living, intellectual principle from whom another living, intellectual being takes life, that life which the mother first possesses. The blessed water of Baptism, then, is a symbol of Our Lady, Our Mother. To be a Christian is to be born again of Mary and the Holy Ghost.

THE LESSON OUR GENERATION MUST LEARN, therefore, is that their art, "culture," is an abomination before God because it denies the principality of His Blessed Mother. Where Mary is Immaculate in her Conception, we are filthy, conceived in sin, until we are made clean through Her. Where She brings forth living likeness of Herself, the Saints who are Her ornaments, we bring forth those abominations of pride which we would glorify by the stolen name of culture. For when you look at the history of art (including technology into which science has degenerated because it has lost its speculative principle), what do you find? A progressive deordination from its proper end, until today the sincere, misguided lovers of beauty and truth stand aghast at the filthy outpourings of the fine arts, just as they are transfixed by fear of those monstrous children of "science" which threaten to destroy their makers. What is the lesson here, if it is not the Mercy of God calling us back to Him for all our perversity? And not calling us back merely, but as prodigal children to whom He would give His Mother as He had never given Her before — if only we will learn and confess we have gone astray, that our integrity is a living contradiction of Mary, Whom He would give us.

OR LET US SAY IT THIS WAY: THE IMMACULATE Conception, Mary conceived without sin, is the beginning of that conception and birth of Christ which was without loss of integrity. Purity makes us whole. But having given up Mary, the source of our purity, our lives are without integrity. We have become adorers of our own work because we have forgotten Mary, Whose Work alone is Adorable. And we have no middle ground now. For now it is manifest, by the very filthiness of our works, who the workmen are. Integrity, therefore, is Mary.

But here is the difficulty. A short while ago a holy Jesuit priest told me of a certain Capuchin Monk*, a man of extraordinary gifts and powers, who lives somewhere in the south of Italy. When he was asked what was the most vicious and characteristic sin of our time, he said, "hypocrisy." There was no question in his mind. And when I heard the charge, I was puzzled. I had thought of impurity, as Our Lady of Fatima had told the children more souls were lost through this sin than through any other; I had thought of sins against Faith, against Hope, sins of pride; but hypocrisy as the root of these had never struck me. And yet, the more I pondered it, the more I saw how right the charge was. Particularly, I thought how terrible was the scourging of men in our times. Then I thought how necessary this violence must be since God in His Mercy permits it. Next I thought how hardened the hearts of men must be to make this violence necessary. It is not the hardness of a sinner who knows he is a sinner; it is the hardness which denies the sin, which no longer sees the sin, that hardness which was most abominable to Our Lord (as my Jesuit friend observed), the hardness of hypocrisy.

I THINK NOTHING SHOWS FORTH THIS CON-temptible hypocrisy more than psychoanalysis. I do not mean that technique, ordered by charity, which seeks to manifest and overcome those hidden fears and attachments which prevent a happy life. I mean that doctrine inspired by Freud, to which the apparent majority of analysis is committed (I do not mean that they understand it), a doctrine which seeks to cure the soul by the denial of sin. By it, the

---

* Presumably this is in reference to Padre Pio of Pietrelcina (1887–1968). —Ed.

very notion of God is made a monstrosity, a "projection" of our natural father whom man "creates" out of his adult fears in order to perpetuate the protection of his infancy. What in fact does this doctrine teach? That sin is only the extension of childish fears of punishment. The only successful therapy, then is one which rids the conscience of this sense of sin, and thereby removes any "guilt feeling." Therein lies human happiness, to deny any superior law which would limit and measure human action.

This doctrine, moreover, is significant for us not as an isolated error, but like communism, because it is an error which consummates the progressive blunders of our history. That too explains why both these doctrines are as powerful as they are. It is not the hypocrisy of psychoanalysis outside of you and me that is significant; it is the way they operate *in us*, in our love of that culture which begot it. I think it is helpful to see it this way, that God raises up such teachers as Freud and Marx, who, by their very genius, and integrity, could teach us whither our own principles are leading. But I am afraid that so far we only regard them as the Pharisees regarded the woman taken in adultery.

That is why, as I think, we are not yet ready for the teaching of Our Blessed Mother, because we are still convinced of our good intentions; we are hypocrites telling God we would give Him everything, when the one thing He wants, *ourselves*, we will not give Him. And we do not want to see that we will not give Him that. That is why we are so "neurotic," because we are living a lie, trying to convince ourselves that we are acceptable as we are, knowing that we are not, trying to rely on a purity which we know we do not possess, yet saying innumerable Hail Marys with our lips, desiring to become Her child, the fruit of Her Immaculate Conception, yet holding on to our last breath to our own conceptions. If we would overcome the world, let us dare to look at this false mercy in which we hope: the work of our own hands, that lie which is destroying us, in order that we may embrace Our Mother, the true Mother of Mercy. For She is one person. This Mother of Mercy Whom God has given us, and She Who alone has crushed the head of the serpent.

* * *

I HOPE CAROL, THIS WILL HELP TO COMmunicate something of what Our Lady wants us to understand of Her in relation to contemporary teachings. As I was reading it over to Charleen, I had the feeling that it wasn't quite finished. This, I thought, was what Mary wanted to be understood, that our whole culture was founded on a conception of mercy which denied God and denied truth, whereas a living devotion to Mary had to be founded on truth. Men were in fact seeking mercy, but in a lie which denied God. Because men have been so viciously indoctrinated, they see truth as a denial of charity, thus making themselves victims and dupes of a specious mercy which will destroy them. if we can learn to root this out of ourselves, asking Our Mother to teach us, then we may be certain that we shall be able to show others where true mercy lies, IN MARY.

HERBERT THOMAS SCHWARTZ, T.O.P
Georgetown, September, 1946

MEDITATION IN MID-MANHATTAN....

Parable of Two Cities

IF IT HADN'T BEEN FOR COUNT CIANO (God rest his soul) and his book on Mussolini (God also rest his soul), these few words wouldn't have been written.

I had been reading the Count's diary in a Rockefeller Center Building recently when I suddenly remembered a conversation of years ago. A friend and I had been discussing the figure of Atlas holding up the world, that Rockefeller Center statue which faces St. Patrick's Cathedral. My friend told how agitated her father had been when he first saw it. He thought it looked like Mussolini and wondered if the architect or sculptor had planned it so by way of expressing contempt for the Catholicism across the street. He had even sent a flaming letter to the Center's owner about it. Until the morning of my meditation I had not remembered to investigate the supposed likeness, but now I was moved to have a look. Sure enough, Atlas did bear a resemblance to the late dictator. Ironically his head was cast down as if a trifle ashamed.

For all that I did not believe the resemblance to be deliberate, my mind started on a funny train of thought.

Here was Rockefeller Center, symbolizing the peaceful unity of all nations of the world through art and commerce. What was especially remarkable about so costly an undertaking was that it actually did reflect the ideals of one family, almost of one man. What John D. Rockefeller, Sr. had made possible by the fabulous amount of money he made in oil, his sons were using to build a sort of world religion of humanitarianism. The Rockefellers had even planned a world religion chapel — without benefit of dogmas. John D. Rockefeller, Jr. is the angel of the purse for the World Council of Churches. On one of the Center buildings you can see a ploughshare with two swords stuck through it and the number of Isaias' text is next to the symbol. All very biblical and prophetic.

The Center has its International Theater, which was not long ago offered to the U.N.O. as a site for the beginning of world government.

Communications link men together. So it is fitting that the Center is Radio City, beaming out programs to the whole world. The latest in television is being worked out in these buildings. *Time*, *Life* and *Fortune*, those ubiquitous magazines, have their offices in one of the towering skyscrapers. In another, the Associated Press relays an endless stream of world news by wireless, teletype and wirephoto. Even Tass has its offices there.

Goods from all over the world are sold in the multitude of "nation" stores scattered through the buildings. Tourist agencies entice you to every land and sea. It houses the consular offices of many nations. Quite logically it has become a mecca for the multitudes of visitors who daily pour into New York.

Then I thought of that other fellow whose name is *Rock, Peter,* and his church across the way from the Center. This fellow has many followers, little rocks you might call them, or better still rockettes.

This man called Peter presides over this church through the auxiliary aid of Pope Pius XII and Cardinal Spellman and he also is identified with oil, with a very holy oil which in

Greek has come down to us as Christ. Strange parable — two oils fighting for men's souls.

Peter, too, is a man of faith, or was until he reached Heaven. We call that vision faith and his rockettes possess that vision too. With it they see not only the world and its wonders as does television, but God also, only now through a glass darkly, while in this land of passage.

Peter also is much interested in news, the Good News of the Gospel. He has his wireless system, prayer, and his messengers, angels.

And of course Peter's Church is a world church too. It is the universal church, as its name implies. Were men really trying to set up a rival to Peter's Church here across from his cathedral? Or was Rockefeller Center a symbol of a more widespread and unconscious effort to unify the forces of Mammon into a universal religion?

I shook myself out of my reverie. A man's thoughts can run away with him. I turned down Fifth Avenue, startled momentarily by the first sign that caught my eye: *Grace Line.*

ARTHUR SHEEHAN
New York City
August, 1946

INTEGRITY: October, 1946

Mr. business went to Mass,
    He never missed a Sunday.
Mr. Business went to hell,
    For what he did on Monday.

The Frustration *of* the Incarnation

OR

THE NEED FOR A REINTEGRATION OF THE NATURAL AND THE SUPERNATURAL ORDERS[1]

ASK ALMOST ANY NON-CATHOLIC WHAT he thinks "supernatural" means and he will refer vaguely to crystal gazing and ghost stories. Ask him for his concept of a holy man and he will blush slightly, restate the question to refer to a "good" man and describe an ideal not essentially different from the ancient pagan ideal of a just and virtuous man. His highest admiration is reserved for Abraham Lincoln; he would be scandalized by St. Catherine of Siena or Benedict-Joseph Labre. In short, outside the Catholic

---

[1] The following informal distinction can be made between the several orders: *Natural* is what is proper to anything in the created order. (examples: reason, as natural to men; nutrition as natural to men and animals); *Supernatural* (above the natural) refers to God's nature, present in the world through grace, because of the Incarnation.

A further distinction is made in theology. *Preternatural* (beyond the natural) designates what is natural to the angels (including the fallen ones), but which is ordinarily beyond us. Our first parents had some preternatural gifts (integrity, immortality and impassivity), but men do not now have such powers, save exceptionally (as levitations).

Church the presence of Divine Life in the world has been almost totally forgotten. A surprising number of people have never even heard of the Holy Eucharist. The words "mystery" and "mysticism" have fallen into discredit. Penance awakens a shudder, sacrifice is misdirected, miracles are disbelieved *a priori*, and the Gospels are grossly distorted. This state of affairs has gone so far that a book like "The Human Life of Jesus" by John Erskine (which is blasphemous) can be chosen as "The Religious Book of the Month."

This situation is reflected in the Church by an artificial separation by the faithful of the supernatural order and the natural order; a separation of their sacramental lives from their daily lives and work. It is the true contemporary schizophrenia.

From this source flows the popular chant, "what's wrong with *that?*" which is used for a justification for everything from jukeboxes to taking a job purely for the financial rewards involved. The assumption back of this popular gauge of morality is that the only connection between the natural and supernatural is one of remote and general intention. The exponents of this theory reason that as long as what they do is naturally good (often enough it is naturally bad and the Catholic does not know it), and as long as they make a morning offering, everything they do is meritorious and they are leading supernatural lives. It is true that such actions when they are good, being formally directed to a supernatural end, are in so far useful for salvation. They remain, however, intrinsically natural. A religious life which stops there is frustrating the Incarnation. It is as though one were to say, "I will do my eating for God, but it isn't possible that that could make any difference in my diet," or, "I'll offer my work to Christ, but the fact that Christ became man is irrelevant to the telephone company I work for."

Another obvious effect of our separation of the natural and the supernatural is prevalent in social action. We tend overly to preach the natural law, especially in matters of social reform and economic planning. The reasons are obvious. In the first place, all men, whether Catholic or not, are bound by the natural law and capable of discerning it. Therefore, it forms a basis on which we can operate with non-Catholics in matters economic, political and social. Certainly we need to cooperate with all men of good will, even before we succeed in converting them, if we do. But it seems that the harder we urge the natural law, the more difficult it becomes to get all men to agree on it. See, for instance, how many men fail to discern the necessity of private property, or the existence of the soul.

Another obvious reason for preaching the natural law is the urgent necessity for reform in the purely natural order. The papal social encyclicals deal at length with social justice, universal human rights, economic reorganization and other problems on the natural plane. Yet not one of them rests matters on the natural level; all urgently advocate the fullness of Christian life. The great encyclicals, for instance, say over and over again, "Seek ye *first* the kingdom of heaven and its justice," yet one seldom hears it quoted when speaking of these letters. Or again, have we forgotten that Pius XI, in *Quadragesimo Anno,* goes out of his way to explain that we cannot be one with the earth-bound Socialists, even when they happen to be right on a particular issue?

"Those who wish to be apostles amongst the Socialists should preach the Christian truth *whole and entire,* openly and sincerely, without any connivance with error."

IT IS EASILY POSSIBLE TO OVEREMPHASIZE THE natural order, so that the Catholic Church becomes known as the Church that recommends a corporate state, or that defends private property, or that urges a living wage, or favors the land movement. All these things the heathen do also, and often better than we. The most successful folk dances in New York are run by the Communists. Cooperatives are still the glory of the Danes, and credit unions are anyone's baby. In what sense is a program *Catholic* which can be subscribed to as well by Socialist agnostics and followers of Gandhi? It may be good, and yet not good enough either to bring us finally to God or to save an earthly society.

And what about our propaganda with non-Catholics? Are we trying to convert them to the Church via private property and the natural dignity of human being? What right have we to assume that they are not aching rather for the remission of their sins and a share in the Divine Life, and that these might now prove a much greater attraction?

In any case, we are badly in need of considering the natural and the supernatural orders to see if their relationship is not closer than, and different from, that which we ordinarily think.

THE SUPERNATURAL IS NOT THE CULMINATION OF THE NATURAL

The natural order does not get any nearer to the supernatural order, no matter how splendid it becomes. A man does not, by becoming more and more zealous in the practice of natural virtue, grow into supernatural life. Whether or not he disposes himself for supernatural life is another matter in which natural virtue's role is only the negative one of removing implements. If he does, supernatural life comes not through his own efforts, but through baptism, by water, blood or desire. Who can say whether a Vassar graduate is a more likely candidate for grace than an Alcoholic Anonymous? Who can say that a learned man is nearer to Divine Life than an ignorant one? Or that life in the suburbs disposes more for grace than life in the slums? Or that a strong-willed matron is a better candidate for conversion than a weak-willed financial failure? One can argue that, other things being equal, what is naturally good forms a better basis for leading the life of grace, once grace has been received, but not that it of itself pulls heaven earthward. The natural as natural has no claim whatever on super-nature and does not even lead in the direction of it. In the matter of disposing oneself to receive grace it cannot even be argued that good natural conditions of life are especially valuable, because the supreme disposing condition is humility, and humility does not ordinarily characterize worldly success. As a matter of fact, natural despair is very close to supernatural hope, in the sense that it is a disposing agent. Alcoholics Anonymous make use of this fact without being aware of the theology involved. They like to catch their drunks when under the humiliation of an especially disastrous bout, and remind them of how powerless their own good intentions are. "Cast yourself on God, or what you know as God," is their recommendation. "Admit that you cannot reform of yourself and ask God to do it for you."

Another example of the power of humility to receive grace is given by Leon Bloy* in the case of his one-time mistress. He tells that she was converted from a life of prostitution to

---

* French author (1846-1917) and Catholic convert whose works were instrumental in the conversion of Jacques Maritain, Joris-Karl Huysmans, and George Roualt. Some of his novels include *Despairing* (1887) and *The Woman Who Was Poor* (1897). — Ed.

a high degree of sanctity in a very short time, owing to her complete abandonment to the will of God.

WHAT IS TRUE OF INDIVIDUALS IS ALSO TRUE OF society. Higher wages, clean washrooms, just laws for Negroes, good housing, farm life, folk dancing, washing machines, parks and clean government, do not *of themselves* tend to Christianize society. They are just good things which improve society in the natural order. The very thought of a society in which these things were regarded as the *summum bonum,* as ends in themselves, and in which they had been largely achieved, would make one yawn or reach for a drink, according to one's temperament. Life would be hygienic boredom in a garden suburb. It would be partial living and quiet desperation. Wherever a semblance of this has been achieved; wherever men have regarded material niceties as ends in themselves and have achieved a comfortable modicum of them, the same phenomena have been observed. Whether in pre-war Scandinavia, in American suburbia, or in a grandiose housing project, behind the lifeless façade of material luxury, is drunkenness, insanity and suicide, going up and up.

All the department stores and cancer committees and country clubs and refrigerators lumped together will not bring us eternal life. In the absence of these things we hope in them. In the possession of these things we know our own despair. Herein lies the explanation for Communism's appeal to the rich and intellectual (those classes with a surfeit of natural goods). Men have a passion for the absolute. Communism is an absolute, a religion. It is not a new egg beater, but a cause to die for. It does not demand five dollars down and ten dollars a week, but blind and unswerving loyalty.

The Frustration of the Incarnation

EVEN WHAT IS NATURALLY GOOD CANNOT BE NATURALLY OBTAINED

An earthly paradise is not for us fallen creatures. Because of original sin we cannot attain it; because of grace and redemption, it would not satisfy us if we could.

For the individual human being (unbaptized) who has reached the age of reason there is no such thing as an extended state of natural goodness. Not being in the state of grace, he will inevitably fall into mortal sin before very long. This is one of the Church's official teachings on grace. "Man in the state of fallen nature, not healed by habitual grace, cannot long remain without mortal sin."[2] Catholics are not affected by this, of course, because since they are validly baptized, they are not candidates for *natural* goodness anyhow. They have been healed by habitual grace, at least once. But what about our non-Catholic friends, whom we blithely assume to be as good as gold and ready candidates for Heaven (which, incidentally, relieves us of the necessity of being apostolic among them)? Few of them are validly baptized these days, since the proper intention is lacking among liberal Protestant ministers. Therefore, they cannot be assumed at random to possess supernatural life or, in view of the above pronouncement, to be naturally good. What chance is there, then, that they will be able to produce a naturally good society? For you can extend the principle. What one man cannot do without the light and help of grace cannot be done by an aggregate of men with a similar deficiency.

We could have derived the same conclusion from a look around us. We know that naturalism has long been the

---

2 II Council of Milene, can 3. (Denz., No. 103), Coelestine I, "Indiculus" (Denz., No. 132).

predominant philosophy of Western society and now prevails almost universally. No one can deny that Western society is in an unprecedented mess. Isn't this because we have been trying to run it without grace?

We no longer open our peace conferences "in the Name of the Father and of the Son and of the Holy Ghost." From having made an unjust and unwise peace after the last war, we are quite unable to make peace at all after this one. We no longer count marriage a sacrament, and cannot even preserve contractual marriage. It is considered indecent to talk about eternal truths, so we have the curious phenomenon of having nothing really important to say, with magnificent instruments for saying it. Considering health an end in itself, we are quite unhealthy. Refusing to fast, we haven't the strength to resist black markets. Every single branch of our society is sick.

There are a few voices calling for a return to God and to the life of grace. Most reforming voices, however, are still crying for a reform in the natural order. Let's re-arrange this, elect him, divide the spoils this way, and build better school buildings. *Let's appropriate ten million dollars for psychiatrists, and three million for brotherhood, and eight million for cancer. Let's build ten thousand housing projects and set up a commission for holding down excess profits, and examine the kitchen sinks of all restaurants, and clean the teeth free for all school children under ten.*

Americans are full of good will and zeal and plans. They are also more devoid than most people of a sense of the supernatural. The salvation of America will depend not on converting Americans to the idea of goodness and unselfishness. They take to it quite readily. But they must be converted to a sense of the life of grace, a desire to do penance, a love of solitude and quiet, a respect for contemplation.

GRACE PERFECTS NATURE

The statement that grace perfects nature does not mean that nature has to be made perfect before you can top it off with grace. It means that the perfection of nature is only to be obtained, and preserved, through the action of grace. Natural remedies for natural defects will be effective locally and occasionally, as witness the salutary effect of army discipline on weak-willed young men, up to a point. But without grace, what is naturally good tends to become naturally bad, and what is naturally bad tends to become perverted. Without grace men fall into sexual license and, when that is widespread, into unnatural practices. And when whole cities are sunk in lust, as is now the case, how can widespread purity be restored? Only through grace. It *looks* as though it would be sufficient to clean up the news stands, censor the movies, warn about venereal disease and increase the police force. It isn't. Only grace can restore the harmony of our natures. Only with supernatural help can we control our concupiscence. The natural remedies follow along, but by themselves are insufficient.

It all goes back to Adam and Eve. The harmony of their natures prior to the fall was contingent on the fact that they were subject to God and possessed supernatural life. Because of this, their lower natures (and lower nature generally) were subordinate to their higher natures. It was when they disobeyed God that everything got out of hand. Consequently, the key to our control of ourselves and the world is our corporate subordination to God.

The further men get away from God, the worse become our troubles. The worse our troubles become, the more irrelevant God seems, whereas the truth of the matter is that the more imperative it has become to have His help. We may soon reach the point where it will be too late to save all those naturally good things we cling to with such persistence, when we can only save ourselves by the mass manufacture of hair shirts.

SOME MISTAKEN NOTIONS

It must be borne in mind that the supernatural life is not wholly identical with the pious life. It is hard for some people to see how grace can save the world because they think of grace as something apart from, and not affecting, daily life. This is mostly because of stopping short at the "there-is-nothing-wrong-in-what-I-do-and-I-make-my-morning-offering" sort of religious life. We do not let grace course through us into social life, we do not take our inspiration from the Holy Ghost. The multiplication of devotions, even daily Mass and Communion, will not tell in the life of society unless grace is allowed to mold our *whole* lives. How does one express grace? In everything. The Catholic cathedrals of Europe are grace caught and expressed in stone. Radio City is the spirit of commercialism and man's fancied omnipotence, fashioned in steel and concrete.

A further misconception is that the supernatural has to work within the present social and economic framework. There has been built up a dogma, a sort of phobia, that the present social and economic structure is here to stay; a feeling that God must supernaturalize file-clerking, and wouldn't dare destroy the files; a conviction that democracy is at least as inviolable as Christianity and possibly more so. Under this conception, we Christians are the sprinklers of holy water, who must repair all the little things and query none of the big ones. We must get rid of this phobia so that it will not stand in the way of the Holy Ghost's inspiration. Let us be ready for anything, so long as God wills it.

The Frustration of the Incarnation

Another, and worse, error is the supposition that we can save our own souls apart from society. We have corporately sinned by directing society to ends irrespective of, and often inimical to, God. We need corporate as well as individual reform. Furthermore, we are all in the same boat, a very leaky one materially speaking. Strangely enough Catholics don't, but they should, feel at home in this vessel, as the bark of Peter was never an individualist's paradise. If God intends us to be apostles in the modern world, we shall not be abundantly favored by grace if we run away from it.

REFORM THROUGH THE SUPERNATURAL

A strong injection of the supernatural at any point will act to renew society. But supernatural grace will have to be allowed to do its transforming work. It is most often not allowed in our society. Take the imaginary instance of a relief administrator in the state of grace. Suppose he refuses help to a needy man owing to a residential technicality bound up with the relief law. He may have to observe his rules, but he is certainly not exercising his supernatural gift of charity (unless, of course, he makes his private gesture), and therefore cannot be said to be injecting the supernatural into society just because he is in society and supernatural life is in him.

Suppose the supernatural is allowed to express itself in us, and consequently in society. What would happen? Who can say exactly? The effects of Divine Life are always unpredictably lovely and are forever beyond the capacity of "planners" to anticipate (if they were, by chance, to take such things into account). Besides, it is not for us to inquire too deeply into the workings of God's Providence, for fear of presuming to understand what is essentially a mystery. Still, it does no harm to point out some of the probable consequences in obvious cases.

LET US TAKE PENANCE, AS A TIMELY SUBJECT. IF we could not figure out ourselves that a wave of penance were in order, we could learn as much from Our Lady, for it has been the burden of her several messages within the last century. We are obviously going to do penance, whether voluntarily or not. Europe is undergoing an unprecedented fast, which might be regarded as imposed penance which God has allowed those countries to suffer. If so, we can look forward to something of the sort ourselves, since so far we have done nothing to warrant exemption.

It might conceivably happen that presently, under the terror of atomic bombing, and urged by holy and fiery preachers, possibly over the radio, several million Americans would take to the traditional sackcloth and ashes. It would be an edifying sight. Imagine an army of Franciscan-like penitents filling the highways from coast to coast and refusing to eat anything more tasty than the scraps of old hot dogs left by the Sunday picnickers. Converted psychiatrists might form a special elite of flagellants, scourging themselves constantly for their sins, the while repenting their foolish talk about masochism. There would be bonfires in every city, into which the frenzied citizens could throw their lipsticks, nylons, comic books and cheap literature. The Radio City choruses, clad in long and formless garments, would perform penitential dances to the *Attende Domine,* with the entire audience bursting forth on *quia peccavimus tibi.*

One can easily imagine that such a change of American hearts might move God to the use of extraordinary means to save our country. A legion of anti-aircraft angels, for instance.

However, let us suppose for the moment that we were to do penance less spectacularly and without waiting until the zero hour. It is easy to show that any appreciable amount of mortification could not help but transform the economic and social structure.

Fasting is an elementary and very efficacious form of penance. The Church theoretically demands a considerable amount of it from every able-bodied Catholic. Most Catholics are excused, for one reason or another; and the Protestants have lost the very notion of fasting. One never hears of the food stocks fluctuating during Lent or on Ember Days. They would, though, if even the faithful denied themselves on the specified occasions. Proof is that the fishing industry attunes itself to the Friday abstinence, which we do observe pretty conscientiously.

If we were to fast, first of all there would be less food consumed. That would mean more food for Europe. That would mean better health for us, because as a nation we overeat.

Two slices of bread is the specified fasting breakfast. You cannot work on two slices of the denatured white bread that is currently extolled in the advertisements and grocery stores. The quality of bread and other foods would have to improve, and this improvement would eventually be reflected in a decrease of degenerative diseases.

YET OUR SPIRITUAL HEALTH IS WHAT WILL PRImarily benefit from fasting. We would see conspicuous improvements. Take the matter of black markets. They are scandalous in America. They are obviously not the handiwork of a few depraved individuals, but bear testimony rather to the self-indulgence of millions of housewives. Mrs. X likes butter. Butter disappears. Mrs. X is tempted to satisfy her longing for butter through illegitimate channels. Mrs. X succumbs. However, if Mrs. X put in fifty or sixty days annually of eating less than she desired, it would be pretty easy for her to pass up gastronomic gratification in deference to the common good. If Americans were able to resist black markets, the economic order would be profoundly affected. Similarly, we would be able voluntarily to eat less on the whole so that other nations could eat more. Who can deny that that would affect international amity? It is useless to pretend that we can do these things for purely natural motives of altruism or enlightened self-interest. The religious motive has the strongest appeal and, therefore, the best chance of succeeding. Lesser motives are currently failing ignominiously.

Fasting has indirect results too. The will, once strengthened, is primed to resist a variety of temptations. For instance, one who fasts does much to overcome temptations to impurity. Jacinta (one of the children who saw the apparition at Fatima) was told by Our Lady in the hospital that it was the sin of impurity that would ruin the greatest number of souls. Any return to purity would have enormous repercussions; it would restore the dignity of women, strengthen the family, and consequently, the state, etc. We are concerned here only to point out that penance is an approach to the problem of restoring purity.

Another simple form of penance is the practice of custody of the eyes; the practice of deliberately not looking at everything that offers. This may sound like a silly or a trivial mortification, but it was obviously suggested by the fact that the eyes are a major avenue of temptation. Practically the whole advertising business rests on that fact. What if women decided, in consequential numbers, not to look at any of the advertisements in the *Saturday Evening Post?*" What if all the Catholics in New York gave up reading subway car cards and instead read pious books or said their rosaries going back and forth to work? What if several hundred thousand women declined, say as an offering for peace, to look in any store window during Advent?

What if all pious societies of men refused for a year to look at any women's legs? What would happen to the sale of nylons? Very much of this sort of thing and the whole economic system would be threatened.

AND SO IT GOES. PENANCE MIGHT BECOME POPular. People might cut down on the number of clothes they exposed, throw away half their furniture, take the rugs up from the floor, glory in china that doesn't exactly match. They might do all these things if they discovered that it would free their minds for much more important spiritual things. It is just barely possible that they might. And if they did, the whole direction of our society would be changed.

PETER MICHAELS
(CAROL JACKSON)
New York City
Feast of St. Augustine, 1946

INTEGRITY: October, 1946

"Marriage should be fruitful,"
    Mrs. Smith was wont to say.
Since putting cash in real estate,
    She turns the fruit away.

Are You Ashamed of the Gospel?

THERE ARE TWO WAYS OF PRESENTING Catholic social doctrine. One is to present it integrally, precisely as it is contained in the authoritative documents of the Church. The other is to present it selectively, carefully emphasizing what is acceptable to contemporary ears and maintaining a disingenuous silence about the rest.

The currently fashionable social ideology is a certain variety of liberalism, represented most concretely perhaps by the New Deal legislation of the 1930's. It is a sort of democracy which, especially during the war years, has shown definite tendencies toward *statism*. It is a temptation, therefore, to present the Church's social doctrine in such a way that it takes on a specious appearance of liberalism. To do this is not altogether difficult; for Catholic teaching favors the principle of collective bargaining, sane social legislation, interracial justice, effective international organization, and many other policies which liberals also support. By putting exclusive emphasis on such measures a Catholic can curry favor with the liberals and even gain a certain tolerant acceptance among them.

To preach the Gospel selectively, however, implies a shocking intellectual arrogance. After all, what right have we to pick and choose among the doctrines of the Church? None at all, quite obviously! Yet the temptation is besetting and even sincere and earnest Catholics may, consciously or unconsciously, hedge a bit in preaching the Church's social doctrine to a reluctant modern world. Therefore it behooves all of us to examine our consciences. Do we dare, for example, to present such doctrines as the following frankly and emphatically to our incredulous liberal contemporaries?

(1) THE UNION OF CHURCH AND STATE. No doctrine is more repugnant to the liberals and no doctrine could be more clearly proclaimed by Rome. Pope Pius IX condemned the proposition, "The Church is to be separated from the State and the State from the Church"[1] Union, of course, does not mean fusion; but it does mean among other things, that the State should actively favor the Catholic religion, that it should bring its laws into harmony with ecclesiastical legislation, that it should help the enforcement of the latter, when necessary, by civil penalties, and that it should lend financial support to the Church when ecclesiastical revenues are insufficient.[2] Of course this ideal condition of affairs is too much to hope for in the United States. We rightly rejoice in the freedom which the Church here enjoys. We are entitled to consider the American system the best system practically possible under the circumstances. But we are warned by Pope Leo XIII that "it would be erroneous to draw the conclusion that American practice represents the ideal status of the Church or that it would be universally lawful or expedient to divorce and separate State and Church as is the case in America."[3]

(2) FREEDOM OF WORSHIP. The second of the "four freedoms" is "freedom of every person to worship God in his own way — everywhere in the world."[4] But Pope Leo XIII spoke of "that freedom in individuals which is so contrary to the virtue of religion, namely, *freedom of worship* as they

---

[1] *Syllabus of Errors*, December 8, 1864, proposition 55
[2] For a brief but authoritative treatment of the question see, E. Valton, "Etat," *Dictionaire detheologie catholique*, 5:879-905.
[3] Letter, *Longinqua*, January 6, 1895, *Acta Leonis*, 15:7.
[4] Franklin D. Roosevelt in an address to Congress, January 6, 1941.

call it"[5] and Pope Pius IX condemned the proposition, "In our day it is no longer expedient to recognize the Catholic religion as the sole religion of a state to the exclusion of all other cults whatsoever."[6] The difference between the Catholic and the liberal position is quite obviously striking.

(3) THE SIN OF INFIDELITY. Liberals claim for every man the right to think as he pleases about the Christian revelation; but in Catholic eyes infidelity is the greatest of all sins excepting only the direct hatred of God.[7] In our confused age it is easy to fall into infidelity through sheer ignorance and therefore we should be extremely reluctant to judge the guilt of individual non-Catholics; yet this does not affect the fact that infidelity, considered objectively in itself, is heinous. It is a sad commentary on the theological backwardness of the day that many good Catholics who are deeply shocked at such lesser offences as murder or sexual perversion can yet preserve their equanimity face to face with the greater sin of infidelity.

(4) FREEDOM OF SPEECH. Such freedom, in an unrestricted sense, is a cardinal dogma of liberalism; it constitutes indeed the first of the *four freedoms*. Catholics too, defend the right of all men to preach the truth and to discuss freely and temperately all genuinely doubtful matters. But there exists no natural right to propagate falsehood, for example, to attack the Christian revelation. "If unrestricted license of speech and writing granted to all," wrote Pope Leo XIII,

5 Encyclical, *Libertas*, June 20, 1888, *Acta Leonis*, 8:229. The whole encyclical is a searching and well-balanced criticism of liberalism and deserves to be more widely known.
6 *Syllabus of Errors*, proposition 77.
7 St. Thomas, *Summa theologiae*. II-II, q. 10, a. 3 and q. 34, a. 2. Infidelity in the broad sense includes also the sin of heresy; but in our day most non-Catholics are infidels in the strict sense also since only validly baptized persons can become heretics.

"nothing will remain sacred and inviolate."[8] The Church therefore defends the censorship and prohibition of books by ecclesiastical action and her general prohibitions are much broader than most Catholics realize. Read Canon 1399 in the *Code of Canon Law* and you will see what I mean.

(5) CONSCIENTIOUS OBJECTION. Catholics, as good citizens, have the strict duty of defending their country in a just war even to the loss of life itself. If, however, a Catholic knows with moral certainty that a given war is unjust he has the equally exigent duty of refusing to serve. All Catholics, then, are bound to uphold the principle of conscientious objection in this sense whether they agree or disagree with the conscientious objectors of this or that particular war.[9] In spite of their emphasis on individual liberty, many liberals have been more than a bit hesitant in defending conscientious objection. Their love of personal freedom and their tendency toward *statism* worked in opposite directions, it would seem.

(6) PUBLIC SCHOOLS. Pope Pius IX condemned the proposition, "Catholics can approve that system of education which is divorced from the Catholic Faith and from the authority of the Church and which is concerned, exclusively or at least primarily, with merely natural knowledge and the purposes of terrestrial society."[10] A point which Catholics often miss is that the system of public schools is not only unsatisfactory for Catholic children but that the whole

---

8 *Libertas, Acta Leonis*, 8:233.
9 The present writer agrees with the position of the conscientious objectors who held that our entrance into the late war was morally unjustified. This, of course, is merely a personal opinion since Rome did not pronounce decisively on the justice of the war while theologians and ecclesiastics tended in general to support the cause of their respective countries.
10 *Syllabus of Errors*, proposition 48. See also proposition 47.

principle of education directed toward a merely natural end is wrong. Here the disagreement with liberals is fundamental.

(7) SUPERNATURAL SOCIAL ACTION. Pope Leo XIII laid down the principle which Pope Pius XI repeated that "if human society is to be healed, only a return to Christian life and institutions will heal it."[11] These words express succinctly a truth which is repeated again and again in various forms throughout the social encyclicals and which is, indeed, absolutely fundamental to the Catholic viewpoint. Merely natural means are impotent to reform society; the specifically Christian, supernatural element must be added. No matter how warmly we support social legislation and collective bargaining, we must remember that the complete solution of society's problems must involve supernatural social action. At the end of his great encyclical on the condition of labor Pope Leo XIII declared that "the well-being which is so longed for is chiefly to be expected from an abundant outpouring of charity"[12] and charity is a supernatural virtue!

(8) THE ROLE OF PRAYER AND PENANCE. Pope Pius XI stated his conviction that "for the evils which afflict the human race today a remedy can be offered in no other way except that all strenuously wage a holy war against the common enemy through prayer and penance."[13] This is a specific application of the general principle of supernatural social action just mentioned. Particularly shocking to the

11 *Two Basic Social Encyclicals* (New York: Benziger, 1943), pp. 36-37 and 172-73. This approved edition of the encyclicals gives both Latin text and English translation.
12 *Ibid.*, pp. 80-81
13 Pope Pius XI, encyclical, *Divini Redemptoris*, March 19, 1937, *Acta Ap. Sedis*, 29:96. Translation from John P. Lerhinan, *A Sociological Commentary on "Divini Redemptoris"* (Washington: Catholic University Press, 1946), p. 113. See his excellent commentary on the passage, pp. 171-73.

modern temper is the notion of social reform through penance. Get out the sackcloth and ashes, boys, and let's solve a few social problems.

(9) THE ROLE OF THE HOLY EUCHARIST. Pope Leo XIII, speaking of the evils incident to the class struggle, "arrogance, harshness, and fraud among the more powerful, misery, envy, and turbulence among the poor," declared that "these are evils for which it is vain to seek a remedy in legislation, in the threat of penalties, or in the devices of human prudence," and went on to propose the Holy Eucharist as the true remedy.[14] His argument was as simple as it was convincing. Since these evils are due to a lack of charity it is logical to turn for their solution to the great source of charity which is the Holy Eucharist. This doctrine, which must be obvious to any thinking Catholic, is utterly meaningless to the typical liberal. Here, even more patently than on most other points, Catholicism and modern liberalism are worlds apart.

On specific issues Catholics and liberals often find themselves in agreement. Therefore they can freely cooperate, for example, in a campaign against race prejudice or in agitating for the passage of good social legislation. It would be a grave mistake, however, to imagine that the agreement is more than superficial. Only in a comparatively restricted field can both parties agree on concrete issues and, even in this field, they support the same measures for different fundamental reasons. Catholics hate race prejudice because it is opposed to supernatural charity; liberals hate it out of a vague humanitarianism. As soon as one peers beneath the surface it becomes completely clear that Catholicism and liberalism are mutually incompatible social philosophies.

---

14 Encyclical, *Mirae caritatis*, May 28, 1902, *Acta Leonis*, 22:126.

To attempt to conceal or minimize this fundamental incompatibility is a serious mistake. We can create a specious impression of unanimity only by systematically withholding many important Catholic social doctrines. No one has a right to do that; it is utterly disingenuous. It is unfair to keep the general public in ignorance of the full Catholic position. For why should a man become interested in the social doctrine of the Church if he receives the impression that social Catholicism is only a mildly variant variety of liberalism? "How are they to believe him whom they have not heard? And how are they to hear, if no one preaches."[15]

TO BE ACCEPTED AMONG THE LIBERALS IS flattering to certain temperaments. Liberals currently enjoy a certain prestige. Liberals are in a position to bestow certain favors on their friends. On the other hand, to maintain the undiluted Catholic position openly and fearlessly is often a relatively lonely task. It requires a certain moral courage. The temptation to water down the purity of Catholic doctrine a bit, at least by passing over lightly its more unacceptable portions, is a very real temptation. Some succumb to it.

This was not the habit of St. Paul. He boasted, "I am not ashamed of the gospel"[16] and no man had a better right to boast. Because he despised all guilty compromise and always refused to hedge, he was mobbed and stoned and scourged and thrown into prison. But neither lash nor sword nor prison bars could shake his utter loyalty to the doctrine of Christ. "Am I seeking to please men?" he asked.[17] The best answer is his heroic life and his heroic martydom.

15 Romans, 10:14.
16 Romans, 1:16.
17 Galatians, 1:10.

No one who preaches the social doctrine of Jesus Christ can hope to please men. He himself, on trial for His life, was charged with being a social agitator.[18] We, his followers, cannot hope for better treatment. "No disciple is above his teacher, nor is the servant above his master."[19] Our Lord promised His faithful followers in this world no higher reward than the cross.

We cannot hope to please men; our sole duty is to please God. To expect to placate the liberals is a mad and guilty ambition. We have no right to dare to be ashamed of the Gospel. St. Paul was not ashamed of the Gospel. The martyrs were not ashamed of the Gospel. The glorious popes of the great social encyclicals were not ashamed of the Gospel. Are you?

PAUL HANLY FURFEY
Catholic University of America
September, 1946

Modern economics
   Would be shot full of holes,
If personnel managers
   Found that workers had souls.

---

18 "He is stirring up the people" Luke 23:5. To stir up is to agitate.
19 Matthew, 10:24.

The Perfect State

PERFECT CITIZENS OF THE PERFECT STATE—
The P.B.C. has the great honor of presenting Citizen X14102 who will give us a brief summary on the historical background of the founding of our government.

THE YEAR 2500 A.D. SAW THE ARRIVAL OF THE Perfect State. For the first time since the dawn of Creation mankind had achieved the ultimate in government — man had created the Perfect or the Secular State.

The advent of the Perfect State was not ushered in with spectacular demonstrations or with bloody riots. No one can state with certainty exactly what chance event transformed the imperfect into the Perfect State, but suffice to say that one day the citizens of the world awoke to the stupendous fact that they were now living in the Perfect State.

It must be stated that sporadic attempts had been made during the ages to create the Perfect State, but it was the people of the Twentieth Century who made the first scientific attempts at its creation. Every schoolboy knows the story of the rise and fall of the great communistic and fascist states of Russia and Germany. These systems appeared outwardly to be at war with each other but essentially and spiritually they were akin.

Their fundamental philosophy, which was in reaction against the individualistic finance capitalism of its day, sought to make the social collectivity the final end of man. Man had no value or dignity of his own except that which the State conferred upon him. His highest duty consisted in finding a place as a cog in the wheels of the omnipotent State.

It is not necessary to go into the history of these social experiments. We know full well that due to certain fundamental inherent contradictions these States collapsed and fell, but they had performed their mission. They had placed mankind upon the right road by uncovering the basic truth that man lives for the State alone and that apart from the State he has no value.

IT IS WELL KNOWN THAT THIS TREND OF AFFAIRS WAS OPPOSED BY THE CATHOLIC CHURCH. In the forefront of reaction it upheld the weird belief that all men are children of God and have a supernatural destiny which the State must defer to while promoting the temporal welfare of the citizens. Once again it sent forth its Martyrs to die for the belief that man has an eternal destiny with God.

Fortunately, for us, the Church failed to stem the tide in the direction of Totalitarianism. The forces of Secularism and Naturalism had done effective spadework in turning the minds of the people away from a belief in a supernatural destiny. They began to look for their heaven upon earth.

The Secular State, which was the forerunner of the Perfect State, directed its first attempts at destroying the influence of the Church. Religious instruction was forbidden in the State Schools under the pretext that the State could not favor one religion over another. From this it was but a simple matter for the State to outlaw Parochial Schools and to force the children into attending its own secular institutions.

The Church defeated in the sphere of education, the advocates of the Secular State directed their attack against the many private charitable institutions. The Catholic Church put up a mighty battle in behalf of the sick and the helpless, but it was of no use. Hampered by legislation and excessive taxation the Church was forced to relinquish, one by one, her numerous institutions.

Euthanasia and birth control became the law of the land. It was decreed that all useless persons were to be mercifully put to death, and that no marriages could take place unless sanctioned by the State. Needless to say the Catholics put up unlawful opposition to these laws with the result that they were cut off from the protection and the bounty of the Secular State.

And because of the consistent and obstinate refusal of Catholics to obey the laws they were all banished to an island in the South Pacific. This island, which they have called Rome, is also the dumping place for all social malcontents who are dissatisfied with living in the Perfect State. For despite the perfect care that we take in eliminating at birth any child who shows a marked tendency toward originality — for we have discovered that intelligent people are liable to suffer from a strange ailment called *dissatisfaction* — yet the human equation is still the weakest link in our society and occasionally a child is permitted to live who upon reaching maturity refuses to take his place in the social collectivity.

IN THE BEGINNING THE DEATH SENTENCE WAS imposed upon such recalcitrant person but our wise State has deemed it fitting to banish these people to a life of incredible hardship and torture. On the island of Rome these people have to take care of themselves. There is no State to tell them what to do at every moment of their lives. On this island people actually have to *think for themselves.*

This having to *think for themselves* is thought by our Perfect Scientists to be the contributing factor to the many mental aberrations that can be observed in Rome. It is pathetic to see the manner in which these people cling to outmoded customs and beliefs. Their principal institution is the Church around which all their activities center. They hold to the belief that the human personality is sacred and that no State has the right to violate it. How utterly quaint! We know that it is only because of our Perfect State that we have any value, and that were the State to collapse we would dissolve into a formless mass of chaos.

Take the case of marriage — as citizens of the Perfect State we know well the value of scientific mating. Not one of us knows who were incubated into the world at the command of our State. It is the State that has given us life and it would be treason to think otherwise.

But not so with the unfortunate people of Rome — they still cling to the old fashioned custom of marriage and raising a family. They are free to marry whom they please and the results of these unions are sometimes horrible. Children actually know who their parents are. And because they do not put to death the mentally deficient and the physically deformed they are saddled as a result with a large number of useless people. They claim that it is a sin to put to death the sick and the old.

But our Perfect State in its infinite mercy has not abandoned these people to their richly deserved fate. From time to time missions are sent there in an effort to win them to our social collectivity. Many of those sent have fallen victim to the strange disease from which these islanders suffer, for it is well known that the disease of *dissatisfaction* is highly contagious. It is for the reason that only trained volunteers are sent there with the message of the Perfect State.

But let us not waste too much time discussing the affairs of these unfortunate people — suffice to say that it should be held up as a dreadful indication of the fate awaiting any individual in our social collectivity who would dare to disobey orders. Let us review briefly some of the great benefits conferred upon us by our participation and life in the Perfect State.

FIRST OF ALL WE HAVE NO RULERS OVER US — the entire collectivity is so delicately balanced that it runs as mechanically and scientifically as the great stars of the universe. We arrived at this admirable state of affairs by eliminating the notion of the soul with its attendant idea that the human personality is sacred. The nonsense of Free Will had introduced into the orderly workings of nature a foreign element which, by interference with the delicate balance of the universe, brought about a great deal of suffering. By the process of eliminating the soul and destroying the passions we were able to create men who could take their places in the great social collective. Men who would find their greatest satisfaction in serving the State.

It is written in the books of ancient lore that in the days before the Perfect State man was created in the image and likeness of God. But in the Perfect State man is created in the image and likeness of the work he is to perform.

This is done by the scientific mating of workers and the proper incubation of babies. The birth of a baby is no longer the result of a chance of nature, but is the result of a long careful process of selection and elimination. Citizens who wish to give a number (babies are given numbers instead of being named after Saints) to the State are carefully investigated and screened as to their background before receiving the necessary permission. The darling test tube numbers are then placed in the incubators where they are raised as perfect workers for the Perfect State. How well this has been accomplished can be seen by the fact that mistakes are no longer made in our society. There are no lost motions or lost workdays due to carelessness. There is no recorded instance of any industrial accident having occurred in the past few hundred years. We can well say that the Perfect State is admirably served by perfect stenographers, perfect cooks, perfect machinists, etc.

For the benefit of my listeners I should like to explain the process by which we evolve a group of perfect workers. Let us take the File Clerk as an example. Her work, we know, is essential to the proper running of an industry. How important it is that her work be flawless! One mistake in filing can cause irreparable damage. Before the Perfect State the selection of file clerks was a haphazard affair. They were chosen from a list of applicants with little thought as to their scientific suitability for the job. Needless to say, many costly mistakes were made. But with the advent of the Perfect State all this was changed upon a proper scientific basis. It was no longer left to chance. A law was passed making it illegal and counter revolutionary for file clerks to marry outside of their class. The children born as a result of their union were carefully isolated and bought up in an atmosphere of filing cabinets and these in turn were mated to file clerks with the pleasing result that by years of selective breeding we have managed to evolve a race of perfect file clerks whose sole duty and pleasure in life is the filing of countless records and who are never known to make a mistake.

The Perfect State

IT IS A PLEASURE TO BE ABLE TO VISIT AN INCUBATOR and see the children being formed according to the image and likeness of the work that they are to perform. In some instances we have been so able to mold the child to fit the machine that it is very difficult to tell them apart. Scientist X302040 has been able to evolve a race of typists so accurate that a mistake is an actual impossibility. These typists are distinguished by extra fine sensitive fingers which are attached to an atrophied body. It is hoped eventually to do away with the body.

By the same careful process of breeding we have been enabled to evolve workers having four hands, and who are quite capable of doing the work of two men. In the early days of the Perfect State we were able to breed housewives with leather skin on their hands so as to be able to open cans without cutting themselves. And it is reported that the Russian Scientist X004500 is working on the breeding of two-headed people on the assumption that two heads are better than one.

PERFECT CITIZENS OF THE PERFECT STATE — WE interrupt this discourse on the history of the Perfect State to bring you a special news bulletin. We are informed that epidemics of dissatisfaction have broken out in various parts of the world. There is no cause for alarm as our perfect scientists will soon isolate these malcontents, and speedy banishment to Rome will be their dreadful fate.

STANLEY VISHNEWSKI*
Maryfarm
August, 1946

---

* (1916-1979) He was the first to join Peter Maurin and Dorothy Day when they founded the Catholic Worker in 1933. — Ed.

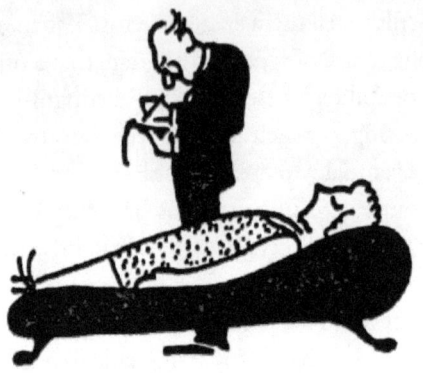

Psychiatrists are a wealthy class,
    Much frequented by ladies,
Since housewives started wanting furs,
    Instead of wanting babies.

The Cross *and* The Dollar

HISTORY IS MOVING RAPIDLY. IT IS VERY hard to trace the underlying direction beneath the innumerable eddies and cross-currents. Each day we hear of some new land where the fire of revolution has broken out. Nowhere, does it seem, is there a quiet, stable country. Even those few far places of tranquility, to which we were once attracted by the travel folders, have tasted war or drink the bitter tea of occupation. The ubiquitous G.I. has energized the lazy lagoon. Cathedral towns show yesterday's scars on their century-old faces. Empty tins marked SPAM lie in the shadows of the Taj Mahal, or half buried in the sand between the paws of the Sphinx. The Royal Road to Romance is under repair. We are locked within the grim citadel of History. History is not a book being read. It is the weary gray faces of people moving restlessly. Scrawled upon walls or carefully printed on placards, in every tongue the words are written: "We Will Not Serve!"

OUR TASK IS TO MAKE SENSE OF ALL THIS. WE are the crew of restoration. The Christian must examine the bits of debris, placing one piece against the other, to discover the nature and shape of the things that must be restored to Christ.

Certain things we know; things that we are sure about. We know that all things get their meaning from God. There is an Order that does exist. This Order is from God, with God, and to God. No other order can make sense unless it is part of their universal pattern. We stand waist-deep in the ruins of today's Tower of Babel. Houses have been built in ignorance of the Universal Architect.

"Unless the Lord build the house, they labor in vain that build it. Unless the Lord keep the city, he watcheth in vain that keepeth it."

AT ONE TIME, SOME MEN GATHERED TOGETHER and decided: "Let every man worship God as he pleases. Let us keep religion out of public life and especially out of business."

These men were listened to. Then one of them said, "Ignore Christ on Monday." Another said, "Do not worship God except in Church." Another said, "Keep the priests in the sacristies." Another said, "My business is my business, and no business of yours, of the priests, of the Church, or of God."

This strange foolishness was accepted. Nations were built according to these plans. As a result, in this tiny piece of His universe, newspapers were printed that rarely mentioned God. Schools were built undedicated to God. The loud voice of Radio was silent of God. God, it was decided, had nothing to do with anything except religion. It became the quietly accepted notion that a religious belief was somehow two or three degrees lower in certainty than a scientific fact. From the amount of words written, lines spoken, and pictures drawn, we might gather that God mattered less than man or the affairs of men.

You and I attended these schools, read these newspapers, and listened to these radios. You and I are part of a society which said that religion is one thing, life is another.

To separate religion from life is absurd. It is impossible. Men do live by principles. Men always will say, "this is right; that is wrong." These conclusions can only be made from principles which are religious. To rationalize our lives apart from God, unresponsive to His Commands, is to bring into being a caricature of reality. We have attempted to run our affairs, our government, our schools, and our business according to our own plan, reserving nothing but private sentiment for that God Who is the Beginning and End of all things. Worshipping our own god in our own way, rather than worshipping the One True God in the manner prescribed by Christ, has brought us to the state where God is, for most of us, a vague inconsequential myth. A private god has become no god at all. A god spoken of in whispered embarrassment is now rarely mentioned.

The consequences of separating religion from life were these:

1) The degeneration of religion into a half-hearted sentimentalism, narrowly self-centered, privately practiced, publicly scorned.

2) The attaching of devotion to material things, and the seeking of wealth as an end in itself.

OUR COLLECTIVE GOD TODAY IS MATTER, NOT spirit. Our religion is woven around idols. Our philosophy is materialistic and these are its marks:

1) It assures us that man is totally and irrevocably earthbound. The immortality of the soul and a life after death are scorned as quaint notions held by the very young and the very old.

2) It tolerates religion as a solace for those who cannot find pleasure in living.

3) It confuses morality with expediency.

4) It devotes itself to the production of trifles which cater to the senses, to the service of which it dedicates the hand and the head.

5) It is always associated with the pursuit of wealth, and the accumulation of pleasures.

6) It is sentimentally self-centered.

All of these are a descriptive definition of materialism. Christ our Lord said, "Without Me you can do nothing."

Materialism is the art and practice of doing much in the pursuit of nothing which abets man's essential happiness. It is the art of cushioning man to the point of anaesthetizing his spiritual discomfort, of deadening his growing despair.

CONSCIENCE IS SILENT WHILE MONEY TALKS

Let me point out materialism to you in that aspect with which you are most familiar. It was not something foreign. It was not one of those awful foreign "isms" you hear about on the radio. It was something as American as baseball, hot dogs, mass production, or the morning toast and coffee. It was intimate with Main Street, with the movies, with the Saturday night out, with the Sunday colored comics. It was the way we lived as a people. Indeed, I can say this, whatever existed in America for the last few generations, apart from materialism, was for that reason considered strange and peculiar.

While under the reign of Industrial Capitalism, the aspect of materialism most familiar to us became that remarkable separation of religious dignity or moral persuasion from every phase of commercial life. The name for this plague is commercialism: the separation of Christ from the market place.

No better introduction to the subject of commercialism can be found than this passage from St. Thomas Aquinas, in which he predicts the inevitable decay of a society dedicated to trade. It is difficult to believe that St. Thomas never lived in New York, London, or any one of our modern bee-hives.

> Again, if the citizens themselves devote their lives to matter of trade, the way will be opened to many vices. For since the object of trading leads especially to making money, greed is awakened in the hearts of citizens through the pursuit of trade. The result is that everything will be offered for sale; confidence will be destroyed and the way open to all kinds of trickery; each one will work only for his own profit, despising the public good; the cultivation of virtue will fail, since honor, virtue's reward, will be bestowed upon anybody. Thus in such a city civic life will be necessarily corrupted.
>
> Consequently, the perfect city will make moderate use of merchants.[1]

During the era of Industrial Capitalism through which we have just passed, the religious, philosophical, and political thinking of the people, rather than molding their economic thinking, was molded by it. The conveniences of the merchant received first consideration. The few times that G. K Chesterton was denied by editors the right to speak his mind, were the times when he had questioned the morality of the economic system. As he so pointedly explained, he might have questioned the existence of God and it would have passed the editor's blue-pencil.

---

1 Thomas Aquinas, *The Government of Princes*. Bk. II, C 3.

In those days, there were still schools, there were still political conventions, and there were still family gatherings, which first acknowledged their allegiance to God before beginning their activities. This was indicative of some good will. Not once, however, have I heard of a place of business which did not spray some satanic D.D.T upon the premises before convening, for fear that there might be lingering from an uncertain past some remnant of Christ and His Charity. That religion be segregated from *commercial* life had always been the prescription of the merchant, and, since in that society the merchant was dominant, religion became divorced from education, from politics, and not unusually from the churches. With unconcern for God's Will in the matter, this fatal separation had been looked upon as a particularly happy arrangement by both the worldly and the pious. Since it was the merchant who was getting the best of the bargain, we were not liable to be informed by his press that this set-up has its gloomy side. That this gloomy side was related to the damnation of souls, was again a fact not liable to give it a place in the headlines. The price of souls, The Life Blood of Christ, had never been quoted on the stock exchange.

IN THAT SECULAR SOCIETY, THE TALENTS which God had given us so that we might continue His Work of Creation and participate in His Divine Son's Work of Redemption, were either buried in the ground or exchanged for a streamlined mess of pottage. A potential El Greco would turn his mind and brush to rendering soups in four colors, so as to line the pockets of a few, and ruin the digestions of the many. The God-given privilege of procreating the race was shelved by many a maid so that she might do vestal duty at the altar of commerce. Christ had lifted man up to membership in Divinity only to have the merchant-society drag him down to the indignity of an automaton.

Of all man's great potentialities, only the lowest were exploited. Money was indisputably god. The banks even made money on Sunday. Since they held (endlessly) mortgages on the churches, many a Sunday instruction had to be shortened in favor of an exhortation on their behalf. How frequently wide-eyed priests lost their evangelizing zeal from continually pouring over the financial books!

Instead of the sweet sound of the Angelus, calling the people to prayer, the shrill factory whistle was heard, causing the people to swear. The time-clock hung where the holy water font should be.

And what had happened to our schools? The children were given the ability to read, to write, and to count. As the child grew older he learned that counting necessary in the art of making change. Later he discovered that reading was the means for escaping from living into the child-heaven of the sports page. If it were a girl, she, through the novel, found entrance into a world where men did something more interesting and admirable than bow to the god of ten per cent. The comics, the box-scores, the stock quotation, the novel; each gravitated to his own field of unreality, thanks to the blessing of literacy. Reading the daily gripe of the columnist became a substitute for doing something about it.

As for the art of writing, the professional letter writer made more money here and with less ability, than he would have among the illiterate masses of India. After twelve years of education the average man used his fountain pen for the main purpose of signing his name. Writers were, as a class, regarded as queer. To all of this, there were many exceptions. Here I am only interested in the rule.

EDUCATION BECAME FOR MOST OF US THE preparation for a job. Since jobs were so uncertain, education became pointless. It was the usual thing to advise the new graduate, "Go out and sell yourself." In the utter confusion to which society had been reduced, it was not too difficult to climb the ladder of success "wrong by wrong."

Remember what St. Thomas said, "everything in the city will be offered for sale." Yes, even the talents, the genius,—and can we separate them, the souls of persons had a price.

OF THOSE FEW SCHOLARS WHO WENT ONWARD into the various professions, fewer still failed to succumb to the persuasion of the dollar. The anarchy and distrust bred by a dog-eat-dog commercialism ridiculed any altruistic search for justice, or selfless service. All of the professions became business. Most of the businesses became rackets. It was not possible for a business man to be honest. It was not impossible for a doctor to be sacrificing. It was not impossible for a jurist to be just. It was not impossible for a teacher to be truthful. With God all things are possible. But it was not customary in those days to be with God.

It would not be fair to leave unsaid or unpraised those men who did maintain their principles through those times. If they had not, then none of us today would have our honorable heritage. Perhaps if we were to review those years from an angle less idealistic than that of Christian principles, we would not be so condemning, but only marvel that anything good had survived. It is to those few heroes that we are indebted for the embers from which we can build a new fire to enkindle the earth.

For the new fire must be soon built. Secularism has failed. Commercialism has failed. There lies before us but one of two alternatives: Catholicism and all its social implications, or totalitarianism with all its slavery.

THE MORNING AFTER

The breakdown of our society has two aspects.

1) The merchant who was unfit to rule because of his natural disregard for the common good, has failed, and his kingdom is falling.

2) Those leaders upon whom government should fall, have become unfit and flabby due to long years of compromise with the dollar, and what is worse, they lack a comprehensive plan for a new order.

Whatever activity still goes on is spasmodic, disorderly, uninspired, and disorganized. Congressmen, university educators, leaders of industry, and the omni-scientists are screeching their last dull nonsense to the body politic which ignores them while madly careening from box-office to box-seat; from the races to the circuses; tossing money about in a last desperate orgy before the lights go out. The optimists among us are placing their faith in those same pitifully empty theories to which our present plight is attributable. The following is a typical excerpt from the notebook of the keep-smiling prophets:

> I feel qualified to predict that this country is in for the most prosperous decade in the history of the world, beginning, if you choose, in this year, 1946. We are going to have more luxuries, more pleasure, more employment, and more production in the next ten years than we have ever had. Only fear and anxiety can prevent it. Americans want to make money, and they will make more in the next ten

years, if they are as brave and faithful as they have always been, than they have ever made before.[2]

Here we find the same old inventory; luxuries, money, production, leisure, while what men are seeking are necessities, self-determination, dignity, inspiration, and virtue.

No Christian could place hope in such a prophecy, even if it were a true prediction. The pursuit of luxuries, pleasures, and the money with which to procure them, if practiced by all of the people, is a certain guarantee of failure for the whole economy.

AFTER ONE HUNDRED AND FIFTY YEARS, THE workers have finally learned to emulate their bosses. There is irony in this and more than a little of retributive justice. On the one hand the merchants and manufacturers had imposed a cruel discipline: WORK HARD, BE ON TIME, BE ACCURATE, BE THRIFTY, BE SOBER, BE ON THE JOB BRIGHT AND EARLY EVERY MORNING. On the other hand, through the happy medium of the colorful advertisement, they taught: EVERYONE CAN OWN A CAR; GET OUT AND ENJOY LIFE IN A HOLLYWOOD TOPCOAT; EAT, DRINK GRIMLEY'S WHISKEY AND BE MERRY; SHAVE WITH SHEEPFATS LOTION AND BE A PLAYBOY; DON'T ENVY MRS. JONES' FUR COAT, PUT A DOLLAR DOWN WITH US; ETC., ETC., ETC.

IN ORDER TO SELL THEIR WARES, THE MERchants had incited greed, covetousness, lust, pride, gluttony,

---

[2] J. A. Krug, Secretary of the Interior, in *American Magazine* for September, 1946.

envy, and sloth. These had become the seven capitalistic sins. Here is the irony: it was only as long as the working man failed to succumb to the vicious persuasion of the advertisement that he would continue to make the reign of the merchant possible. It was only as long as he was not slothful that he would submit to being a producing machine. It was only as long as he was not greedy that he would accept the low wage. It remained only as long as he was not envious that he could tolerate the puffed-up pomp of his money-lord. A generation ago, the husband sired a large family which the merchant used as a soft spot upon which to lay the whip. Now living lustfully and unproductively, the working man has no family to threaten.

The romantic art of the merchant had more persuasion for the worker than did the grim authority of his commands.

Now we find that John comes to work late because last night he was making merry with Grimley's whiskey. Jane is inaccurate in her typing, wondering where she can get the other dollar for her new fur coat. Joe did not show up today. He's out enjoying life in a Hollywood topcoat.

The worker will refuse to be satisfied. As long as he listens to a radio, reads a magazine or newspaper, or sees a movie, he will be reminded that for ten dollars a week more he can secure this new luxury. The employer needs satisfied help. The merchant wants insatiable consumers. People cannot be at one and the same time satisfied and insatiable. The merchant has killed the goose that laid the golden egg. There are now no longer enough suckers to go round. There are now more parasites than there are workers to satisfy them. These are the last days of a society dedicated to the stomach. This is the inevitable morning-after.

THE NEW ORDER

Whether you prefer the term evolution, in describing the changing of the old order, the point is that the change is going on now with lightning rapidity. We are in the midst of transition. Every day sees another of the old gods forced to abdicate. The noteworthy thing is that secularism as a social idea is *dead*. Many of its effects are still with us, but the original impetus is gone. The tenets and ideals of our society are pure and unadulterated materialism. Religion of the supernatural has been displaced by a religion of natural things. Whatever gods the people worship today are concrete, earthy things of clay. These are the gods of the senses: wealth, fame, passion, physical ease.

The gods are being federated. The apostles of Mammon are planning and putting into effect a new order of darkness. In this they will return to the old monotheistic idea. There will be but one god. He will be the Total State.

Lined up against the scheme stands the Catholic Church, the spouse of Christ. The frightening responsibility of bearing arms against tyranny lies completely and irrevocably upon the shoulders of Confirmed Christians.

Would it not be tragic if the last to cling to the tenets of worldliness were those who are heirs to Heaven? Is it strange that the Thing we keep hidden from our associates, as if in shame, is the Bread for which a hungry world is searching?

THE PRESENT WIDESPREAD DISSOLUTION MUST BE AN OCCASION FOR INTENSE MILITANCE ON OUR PART. There is no excuse today for part-time or free-lance Catholicism. Due to our negligence, the atrophying influence of secularism has sadly neutralized the Christian dynamism of our lives and of our Catholic institutions. Even when we do good things, we do them in the spirit of the world. The Sword of the Spirit has grown rusty in its sheath. Speaking of Catholic conformists, Father Furfey says:

> They betray their hesitation, not by positively denying any supernatural social doctrine, but by talking as though such doctrines did not exist... They can discuss the sociology of the family by the hour without ever once mentioning marriage as a Sacrament. They can discourse learnedly about the evils of modern war but not from the standpoint of the doctrine of the Mystical Body. It never occurs to them to propose the Holy Eucharist as the fundamental remedy for the class struggle. They remain consistently silent about all those social doctrines which are peculiar to the Catholic Church. Thus they convey the impression that they do not differ basically from materialists in their social thought. No one would gather from their language that there is a sharp antitheses between the viewpoint of Catholics and unbelievers on social questions.[3]

Certainly it is not to this cowardly, half-hearted Catholicism that we are being called by Christ's vicar! It is not to that which is hard or difficult that the Christian is pledged, but to the "impossible." The task to be done today is tremendous. Nothing short of total revolution can restore our world to Christ.

---

3   Paul Hanly Furfey, *The Mystery of Iniquity* (Milwaukee, Bruce, 1944), p. 31.

IN CONCLUSION

The work of Redemption begun by Christ, and continued by His Church, has been set aside by mankind so that men might devote their lives to self-indulgence and the accumulation of wealth. Today the tenets of secularism have been displaced by the dogmas of materialism, marking the last stage of man's journey away from God. The crisis demands that Catholics, if they would save the world, return to an all-out devotion to the spread of their Christian inheritance.

The work of Redemption is accomplished by Christ through the work of His Members. That is the key to the problem. Hence the work must begin at the Altar with the Eucharist, and then proceeding outward from the churches, be carried by the communicant into every nook and cranny of society. This must be done in a cooperative and organized fashion. To this end the Catholic must reform his life, intelligently and with prudence, bringing all his activities into conformity with the apostolate. Men and women must do this work of apostleship at a personal sacrifice, and at what may appear to be the jeopardy of their security, always remembering that the price we should pay for our daily bread is to seek first the Kingdom of God and His Justice.

> The time to start was yesterday.
> Today is the eleventh hour.
> Tomorrow is the Judgement.

ED WILLOCK
Boston
September, 1946

BOOK REVIEWS

IDEAS FOR A NEW WORLD

ESSAYS IN RECONSTRUCTION
Edited by Dom Ralph Russel
New York: Sheed and Ward
1946
Price: $2.50

It is already out of fashion to denounce our times. What further need is there to expose the decay which assails everyone's nostrils? We can therefore turn our thoughts to the more fruitful task of rebuilding. There will probably be a lot of Catholic books on the subject of reconstruction. This, one of the first, is welcome because of its constructive thesis as well as for its several other excellencies. It is a collection of recent English essays on such subjects as science, literature, philosophy, economics and the spiritual revival.

What is most striking about the essays collectively is the intellectual competence of the authors. They usually start by presenting, tersely and precisely, the Church's teaching, or the history of the relevant heresies, or the policies of the government, or some other background information on the matter at hand. It is always excellently done. One recalls especially the comprehensive view of modern philosophical errors in Dom Illtyd Trethowan's "The Reconstruction of Philosophic Thought," and Michael Fogarty's summary of the economic situation in England (as of 1943) in "Catholics and Economic Reconstruction." Nevertheless, while one admires this intellectual competence, one cannot help hoping that never again will all this academic background material have to be waded through. It is not necessarily in this way that one arrives at the Christian truth about contemporary life. For instance, this same essay on economics does not ring true for all its learning. Analysis and conclusions cling depressingly to the natural order. They are neither so fresh nor so penetrating as Eric Gill's view based on personal experience, observation and intuition. Nor half so true, in our estimation. They also compare unfavorably, in the matter of depth of Christian understanding, with a recent parallel effort in England, Adam Doboszynski's "The Economics of Charity."

The most interesting essays in the book are the first two, the last two, and the one on science. Dom Ralph Russell wrote the first two, which consider the general problem of reconstruction. He writes from the integral Christian point of view, with primary stress on the supernatural elements. The last two essays deal competently with Specialized Catholic Action movements. Their two authors, Lieut.-Col. Hon. Anthony Lytton-Milbanke and Father John Fitzsimons (chaplains of the Young Christian Workers of Liverpool) show penetrating understanding of their subjects. When they describe methods, as they often do, they go out of their way to show why the methods suit the problem at hand.

"Catholicism and Science," by F. Sherwood Taylor, is the exploration of near-virgin territory. The author strongly condemns the attitude which regards science as "purely scientific" and without moral obligations saying:

> The principles of modern slaughter were elucidated by men who were concerned with problems

unconnected with war, and are in no way responsible for the devastation of our world. Those who applied these principles to the armament industry had no more than a cool and scientific interest in a mechanical problem, but cannot be held guiltless. They were interested in science, not in killing; they abstracted their work from its whole consequences but this, of course, does not absolve them from responsibility.

ESSAYS IN RECONSTRUCTION makes no pretense of looking beyond the English scene, thus losing some of its value for Americans. However, it will prove useful until we can do as well.

CAROL JACKSON

PAMPHLETS RECEIVED

RACIAL MYTHS by Mary Ellen O'Hanlon, O.P 25 cents each. Quantity rates. Rosary College Bookstore, River Forest Illinois. Terse anthropological study of supposed race characteristics of the Negro.

AND WHO WANTS PEACE, by Eric Gill. Order from David Hennessy, Maryfarm, R.R. 4, Easton, Pa. One free copy to all who write for it. 5 cents each for additional copies. Attractive reprint of an address given on Armistice Day, 1936

Said the politician:
    A man in my condition
    is not in a position
    to question the sources
    of the checks he endorses.

We have rejected
    the yoke that is sweet
    and bowed to the yoke of fear:

We have feared discomfort and loss,
pain of body and mind,
the pang of hunger and thirst;
We have been abject
before the opinions of men;

We have been afraid
of the searching ray of truth;
of the simple laws of our own life;

WE HAVE LOST THE INTEGRITY OF THE HUMAN HEART;

We are the mediocre;
we are the half-givers;
we are the half-lovers;
we are the savourless salt:

Lord Jesus Christ
restore us now
to the primal splendour
of first love,
to the austere light
of the breaking day.

Shine in us,
Emmanuel,
Shadowless Light:
flame in us,
Emmanuel,
Fire of Love:
burn in us,
Morning Star:
Emmanuel!
God-with-us!

Condensed from *Afternoon in Westminster Cathedral*
by Caryll Houselander, taken from *The Flowering Tree*.
Sheed & Ward, Publisher

INTEGRITY

TO SEE — TO JUDGE — TO ACT

:the second issue:

November 1946; Vol.1, No.2

SUBJECT: THE LAY APOSTOLATE

EDITORIAL

E HAVE SENT TO England for some hair shirts (the best ones are imported) as proof against vainglory. Good will is showered on us. Praise rings in our ears. After reading our first issue a golden-jubilarian nun wrote:

"In this world run wild with mischief we have at long last a hammer and sickle of our own."

May others take heed and be encouraged to undertake Catholic ventures. Far too many Catholics are laying waste their daring and enterprise in the world's marketplaces.

The lay apostolate is the general subject of this issue. We have a spiritual crisis in the social order and the laity must necessarily do most of the work of resolving it. The job can be done, as Paul McGuire[*] points out in *There Is A Solution*.

What is the solution? It is the revivification of the Faith in daily practice, for one thing. It is organization and corporate action for another. While many of us slumbered a few have been at work. The most sensational lay apostolic effort in the Church so far has been Specialized Catholic

---

[*] Paul McGuire (1903–1978) was an Australian author and diplomat. He was influenced by the writings of G. K. Chesterton and Hilaire Belloc. He began to write on issues related to Catholic Action through his encounter with Fr. Joseph Cardijn (founder of Jeunesse Ouvrère Chrétienne or the Young Christian Workers). He was also instrumental in the conversion of Carol Jackson. —Ed.

Action, which is functioning in almost every country except our own. Because it is beginning here, at long last, we have devoted a large part of this issue to the movement. We have described again the major techniques (but from a different point of view) in Peter Michael's *The Leaven*. How it has worked in Canada so far is analyzed by Jim Shaw (*Catholic Action in Canada*). Word of its progress in Europe comes from Father Fitzsimons (*The Workers Apostolate*).

Catholic Action even worked in a Hong Kong concentration camp. Father Hessler of Maryknoll tells how in *Apostles in Prison*.

If Catholic Action is the ideal form of a mass apostolate, especial among the workers, it is not the only fruitful direction which the lay apostolic spirit has taken. The United States has been slow to come to Catholic Action, but at the same time has been the home of a movement equally realistic and intense; possibly even more radical. That is the Catholic Worker Movement, which reflects not Catholic America, but the vitality of ex-Socialist Dorothy Day, and Peter Maurin who began life as a French peasant. Together with those who joined them, mostly young men, they practiced the works of mercy personally in Houses of Hospitality and encouraged others to do so also in their monthly newspaper. That the work of so few has, as it does have, an international and profound influence, is evidence of its quality. Dorothy Day describes in this issue some of the ideas and struggles of the Catholic Worker.

The social philosophies of the Catholic Worker, and of the Jocists under Canon Cardijn, have been largely omitted from this issue, and on purpose. We shall discuss these matters at length in subsequences numbers of *Integrity*. We have also omitted mention of many other lay apostolic groups in the United States. Most of them are working for particular objectives, such as the conversion of the Negro, within the general framework of the lay apostolate. We prefer to consider the major social problems separately, and when we can give them adequate space for the comprehensive treatment.

THE EDITORS

There is a Solution

THERE *IS* A SOLUTION TO THE MODERN dilemma. It strangely is in the hands, heart and mind and will of every Christian. The immediate problem is to make enough Christians understand this, understand their nature as Christians, understand the sort of beings they are, the sort of energies they possess.

The Christian is a member of the Mystical Body of Christ. He shares its life. He shares its energies. He shares its functions in the world and its responsibilities.

The Body is by nature apostolic. That is, its nature is to grow in the world, to extend the teachings of Christ. The Christian is thus apostolic also, sharing the nature of the Body as the branches share the nature of the Vine.

THE BUSINESS OF THE CHURCH IS TO CONVERT the world. Thus the business of the Christian is to convert the world. The world for each one is the range of his personal associations and influence: the people he knows. That range is the range of his apostolate. It is there that he can really do something to solve the problems of our time and of all times. It is there that the reformation of the world, the restoration of all things in Christ can be begun. It can be done where we are. It can be done in all innumerable little worlds entered or occupied by Christ through the life of His local members. This is the terrifying responsibility of the Christian that Christ depends upon him to complete the work for which Christ lived and died. The Christian can stop the work of redemption; or he can continue the immediate mission of his Lord. He must do one or the other. There is no neutral position. He is either with his God or against Him. To be passive is to be against Christ. For Christ depends upon the Christians to continue His task. The Christian Body is essentially dynamic. Passivity in its members is a denial of their nature; and a refusal of graces specifically given for the apostolic task.

WE GET THE WORLD WE EARN. WE CAN BE DONE with war, with much evil which besets us; though each individual and each generation must meet again the consequences of original sin: the darkened understanding, the weakened will. Don't we pray daily (and Christ did not mock us when He made the prayer): "Thy Kingdom come, Thy will be done on earth as it is in Heaven." The City of God is not a hopeless dream. The City of God can be created by each one, first in himself and then amongst his neighbors. If enough are true citizens of the City, it appears.

The difficulty of course is that while most of us are ardent to reform our neighbors few are eager to tackle ourselves; that one part of the world which we really can make sure for Christ. Yet quite obviously there is no other sort of reform worth anything. The institutions of men and their societies express the social values and actions of the men who compose or create them. The good society grows from the good in men: the evils of society grow from the evil in men. This is the first necessary step towards understanding the trouble of our times.

The last century has brought the most startling and far-reaching changes in the social and economic history of man. From them have flowed vast consequences for his spiritual and moral life. The pattern of social life which was developed slowly through the Christian Era of the West is now dissolved. Few men have the energy of mind and will to understand these changes. Most prefer to walk among the ruins in the blindness of old mental habits. But somehow enough Christians must be roused.

THE SITUATION OF THE CHRISTIAN NOW HAS only one parallel: the first years of the Church when a few men ran with its good tidings to the world. The early Christian knew what Christians through the comfortable Christian centuries largely forgot: that the Church is essentially missionary apostolic. When Christian beliefs and values prevailed the work of priest and parish was largely to conserve them. The apostolic life of the Church came to be thought of as a remote activity in mission-fields to parti-colored pagans. But now the pagans are of our own color and a swirling sea about us. The mission-field today begins at the church doors. In each once-Christian neighborhood are tasks and adventures unknown to the conservatism which has lost the advancing world; but which would seem familiar to St. Paul and St. Francis Xavier.

Let's look at the facts — while beating our breasts. Christianity was once the CENTER OF GRAVITY of our civilization. Today it is a PERIPHERAL activity. At work, in leisure, in its social, sexual, intellectual interests, the mass of the modern community is almost untouched by Christian values. Christianity is external to the mass, remote, ineffective, unrealized. The Church still has great institutions and massive organizations. They represent partly an inheritance from the past and partly the energies of a minority of a minority. If they obscure our view and understanding of our racial problem now, we should be better without them.

THE PROBLEM IS TO RENEW THE APOSTOLIC SPIRIT. The Church must re-penetrate the mass from which she has been ejected. The mass will not come to her. She must go to mass as Paul went and Xavier and Assisi.

This is the necessity which has produced the Jocists, the Jicists, and the Missionaries of Paris, priests who work in factories and live in lodging houses. They rely on none of the familiar machinery of parish organization. Their parishes are dead or unborn. They reject the snug security in which western societies still (but for how long?) invest the cleric: the dangerous security which too often shuts him off from real knowledge of the forces working in obscure depths of the masses to whom he is an alien. That knowledge has to be won in shops, offices, and factories, at the coal-face and in the washrooms.

Therefore the Pope has called for a lay apostolate to serve at the coal-face, in the factories, in the washrooms, bars, theatres, newspaper offices, kitchens, camps, colleges, in the stews and middens of the world. The actual apostolate must be at most points the job of laymen. It must express itself much less in words than in life lived out. The seed must be planted again within the strange heaving mass of humanity which has succeeded the ancient societies of Christendom. The Christian community must be reborn and regrown within that mass. Desocialized, the mass is straining towards some shape, some order. It must and will find organization, good or evil. Its struggle towards coherence is part of the agony of these times. It accounts for our obsession with politics, with Statism, with Nazism, Fascism, Communism. For Christians the task is to bring to the struggling mass the Christian spirit which *informing* it may restore it in Christian order.

There is a Solution

WE HAVE MUCH DEAD TIMBER IN METHODS OF organization and habits of mind: especially in the habit which regards our chief task as to conserve. The Church is a dynamic not a static institution. It is constantly losing ground or gaining. It cannot be frozen in set forms. There are essentials of its life which the Pope groups under the phrase "the traditional rules of the Church's public law." But beyond these there must now be innovation, invention, enterprise. The talent must be traded and never buried in safe little holes. It must be traded in the human world about us, in the *milieu*. No Christian can escape the responsibility for this commerce with his generation. There can be no retreat from it, no ivory tower. We have each of us only our own times in which to save our souls and they are saved in the life of the Church: which is apostolic.

Those who go to the higher life of prayer and contemplation still have this corporate function. They praise and pray for their generation. Those who stay in the world pray too but they also have the task of renewing in the world the Christian community.

They renew it by growth. The Christian should never fall into the delusion of the mechanists. We may create practical machinery for specific purposes. A United Nations Organization has many uses. But it will not solve the deeper problems of mankind. It may curb the drug traffic, even perhaps one day provide a police force for the world. But it cannot cure the pain in the heart of mankind, the misery, the doubts, the fears, the hatreds which grow from the negation in him of the good. Only Christ can heal and restore and renew the true life of man. But Christ bends Himself to man. He works for men through men. Men are His instruments of salvation for men. This is what is to be a Christian: to be a member one with Christ, persistent in His mission.

The restoration of this sense and its expression through us in and to the world is the answer and the only answer to the world's agony and shame. There is a solution . . . and it is IN US.

PAUL MCGUIRE
London
August, 1946

Frequently in history
    We find the Christian liable
To seek a softer doctrine
    Than the one that's in the Bible.

Catholic Action in Canada

SINCE THE JOCIST MOVEMENT CAME TO Canada in 1932 it has succeeded in breathing life into the J.O.C. blueprint for Catholic Action that it now stands, with thirty thousand militant workers gathered in four hundred and fifty sections throughout Canada, as the paramount example of vital Catholic Action on the North American continent. It has reached this position by a process of healthy organic growth rooted in strict adherence to the basic Jocist principle of the cell technique applied by working people, working among working people, for working people. In a Catholic Action world that is long on architects and short on builders, J.O.C. has won preeminence because it has more builders than architects, and all its architects are builders.

Although statistics are nowhere more futile as gauges of worth than in the field of Catholic Action, there are two factors that give significance to the Jocist figures. In the first place, taken merely as a number, the membership represents almost one per cent of the total French Canadian population. When we consider that J.O.C. members graduate to L.O.C. upon marriage, that young students, professional workers and farmers have separate Catholic Action movements and that French Canada is still to a large extent rural, this figure represents an excellent coverage of the field. Secondly, and most important, this membership was arrived at by organic, individual-to-individual growth and one is only a Jocist in so far as he is a militant lay apostle. This combination of comprehensiveness and intensity, of total number and individual quality, guarantees that Canadian Jocism is a very real influence in the lives of the workers of Canada.

BUT IT IS BY CONTACT WITH THE LIVING REALITY rather than by the reading of records of accomplishment that the true spirit of Jocism and its real worth as a lay apostolate is brought home. The best way of making this contact is by a visit to the Jocist Centrale at 1037 St. Denis Street, Montreal. The atmosphere of this old four-story building strikes the keynote of the whole organization. It is one of sincerity, simplicity, capability, enthusiasm and joy. There is a lot of laughter in the building and somewhere someone is always singing. The dining room is loud with cheerful chattering as the hundred young men and women who make up the staff come tumbling downstairs to serve themselves good plain food on plain dishes placed on long refectory tables. The visitor is at once introduced to everyone at table and is soon drawn into the family atmosphere. He is likely to end his meal to the accompaniment of melodious French Canadian voices singing the folk songs without which it seems a Jocist can't wash dishes.

As the various national leaders are visited in the offices from which they control the national organization — and they control it, Jocist chaplains are chaplains only — a distinct pattern emerges and a great confidence is born in the absolute integrity of the movement. There is a complete absence of that sterile intellectualism which makes so much Catholic activity a futilitarian game. The leaders all young workers from small town factories and city offices, who have shown capacity for leadership and who have volunteered to give some years of their life to full-time work of Jocism.

There is no stuffiness, no pride of position. The young man who puts out a weekly paper of thirty-five thousand circulation has no feeling that he is anything else than a working man working among working men. He is a Jocist, a worker, and that is that. So it is with all the other leaders. Each is the same, each has the same combination of ability, zeal and humility. Each inspires confidence that Jocism is a genuine worker's movement, not a small group imposing its direction upon a mass of which it is not a part. Canadian Jocism in practice as well as in theory works from within. The spirit within the individual, the individual within the group.

This very worker atmosphere may administer some mild shocks to the "intellectual" visitor. If he is a Liturgical Life addict he will be disappointed to find that the Jocist day is not built around the Church's Office. If he is a musician or literateur, his good taste will be offended that the Jocists should unabashedly sing popular songs and write Jocist words to them. (They have actually put apostolic words to Mademoiselle from Armentieres, incongruously preserving the Hinky Dinky Parley Vous chorus.) If this bothers too much, the visitor may do one of two things. He may go over to the student organization, J.E.C. which is up to its eyes, and even over its head, in Culture. Or he may humbly presume that he doesn't know what works with French Canadian workers as well as French Canadian workers do, and let incidentals drift on the sea of essentials ... *bonum ex integro causa*.

JUVENILE DELINQUENCY

Within the Centrale itself there is sufficient concrete evidence of the Jocist success in influencing the workers' environment to drown any petty objections. This is to be found in the Night Shelter on the fourth floor, which houses forty young men including those remanded from the Juvenile Court into Jocist custody and ex-prisoners brought there to protect them from former surroundings. This functions as part of a wider Social Service Department which brings aid to the needy over the full range of family troubles. Like all Jocist services it grew out of one of the annual Social Inquiries and is characteristically Jocist in origin as well as in method. When a Social Inquiry led thirty thousand Jocists inquiring into conditions in their own factories and workshop to SEE that juvenile delinquency was currently one of the most pressing social problems, they were led to JUDGE that an effort should be made to protect the delinquents from their environment, and to ACT accordingly.

The resultant action produced the Night Shelter and all the services that goes with it. At every Juvenile Court session in Montreal, Jocists are represented, three girls and three boys being assigned to this work. The young "criminals" are interviewed before going to trial. When advisable, their remand in Jocist custody is sought, and, such is the Jocist reputation with the judges, almost invariably granted. The boy is then either taken to the Night Shelter or returned to his home. In both instances, the follow-up is typically Jocist. A Jocist of his own age and in his own neighborhood is given the assignment of making contact with him, and influencing him for the better. He informs himself on the boy's habits, joins his activities, frequents his haunts, and forms a natural friendship without mention of Jocism. As friends, they go to the same places, do the same things. Gradually the former delinquent finds himself with a new set of friends and interests. He generally ends up at informal and then at formal Jocist gatherings, often becomes a Jocist and sometimes a valuable leader.

The boy who is brought to the Night Shelter has his Jocist influence, which is never thrown at him as preaching, at hand. He is guided to a job and after a short time moved to a Young Men's Residence, a boarding house in which he pays his own way and has greater freedom.

A similar residence for girls supplies at once the answer to three problems, that of finding living quarters for country girls coming to work in the city, that of the unmarried mother and that of the juvenile delinquent. Since the house is primarily a residence for working girls, unmarried mothers can be brought there and allowed to lead normal lives without any reference to their circumstances. When their condition can no longer be kept secret, the girls are placed in private homes where hospitalization is provided for and proper pre-natal and post-natal care assured. After birth of the child, the Jociste influence continues. If desired, foster parents are found for the child, the mother is encouraged to return to her home or to find a job where Jociste companionship can continue to help her.

THE MARRIAGE APOSTOLATE

Another year of Social Inquiry resulted in the now internationally famous Preparation for Marriage Course. Tied up with this is the much-publicized Mass Marriage ceremony of 1939 and the impetus this display gave to a common misconception of Jocism as a regimentalized mass movement of artificially stimulated demonstrations in the Fascist manner. Whatever may be said about the dignity of marrying a hundred couples simultaneously in the outfield of a crowded baseball stadium, the louder objections voiced against the display were founded on ignorance. They seemed to presume that the show was meant to stimulate the French Canadian birthrate, and that the hundred couples had been rounded up indiscriminately for the occasion. Actually, the young people had followed a year's course of study in the Religious Moral, Physical, Social and Economic aspects of marriage and the event was planned, whether wisely or not, as propaganda for Christian marriage and for Jocism.

That year's work was the beginning of three years of experimentation from which evolved the present fifteen lesson course. The course which has now been followed by some ten thousand engaged men and women (the sexes meeting separately), is eminently down to earth and practical. Each lesson is presented in a four-page printed leaflet ending with a questionnaire on the subject discussed. The study-group method is followed with priests, doctors or psychologist called in for specialized topics. Some such specialized topics are Male and Female Psychology (by a psychologist), Male and Female Anatomy (by a doctor), Sexual Relations, Pregnancy, Childbirth (by a doctor), Reciprocal Adaptation in the First Year of Marriage (by a married person) and lectures by a priest on the Mysticism of Marriage, the Marriage Ceremony, and what is Permitted and Forbidden in Marriage. Other lessons deal with such things as Dates, the Engagement, Economic Preparation, the Trousseau, etc. The course ends with a day of recollection attended by all.

After marriage, a Jocist becomes a member of the Catholic Worker's League (L.O.C.). L.O.C. issues various services for the first year of marriage, including a Budget Service and more detailed discussion of some of the topics discussed in the Preparation for Marriage Course. Since becoming known outside French Canada, these courses have attracted much favorable attention and are now being translated, adapted where necessary, and made available to English-speaking youth.

OTHER ACTIVITIES

Arising, too, from the annual inquiries are the other activities which keep the Centrale's one hundred and five full-time workers busy. One such is the leisure Time Activities Service which directs reading, helps in the founding of local libraries and encourages parties and entertainment in the home. Another is the Veteran's Aid Organization which began as a service to assist Jocist effort in the armed services. A weekly paper, *Le Front Ouvrier*, with a circulation of thirty-five thousand is published from the Centrale. The paper is up-to-the-minute and lively. The title was chosen in keeping with its general policy of being of general appeal to workers rather than remaining a Jocist house-organ. Other needs revealed by the inquiries are met through the Social Service Department. There is a service for maidservants, aimed at providing a Catholic atmosphere for country girls newly arrived in the city and encouraging them to practice an apostolate in their environment. A special service for the sick has its own publication.

Taken altogether, this practical and systematic practice of the lay apostolate in one sphere of the worker's life after another, is decidedly impressive. It offers thought-provoking proof of the validity of the Jocist technique. The Jocist does succeed in living a more Christian life in a non-Christian society and in moving toward his aim: "To help young workers live an integral Catholic life and to influence his environment so that all workers may do likewise."

BUT, CAN IT WORK ELSEWHERE?

Recognition of this success poses a question: "Can the Jocist technique, so successful among workers in Europe and in French Canada, be generally applied to the whole field of the lay apostolate? Can it be successfully applied to other social groups and to other countries of the world?"

Theoretically, the answer can only be "Yes." For the Jocist technique is simply the basic lay apostolate of the individual who informs and forms himself so that he may inform and form other individuals with whom he comes in contact. To this fundamental is added the fact that the apostolic individuals band together in an organization for mutual encouragement, for the interchange and clarification of ideas and the focusing of effort.

Now are there, in practice, any considerations which limit the application of this simple method either to the working class or to the French (or Latin, or European) mentality?

Obstacles to the successful general application of Jocist technique exist on both grounds. But before discussing these, we should like to say at once that the major difficulties at present experienced come from ignoring the basic Jocist principle of organic growth from the individual. Too often, the Jocist blueprint is taken first and the individual impressed into it. We shall return to this point.

As far as application to other social spheres is concerned, we have test cases here in French Canada. J.I.C., J.E.C. and J.A.C. are three Jocist-type organizations. They deal with Independent, Student and Farm Youth respectively. None of them has attained the efficiency of Jocism.

THE J.I.C.

Of the three, J.I.C. is the feeblest and the closest relative of the typical Catholic youth organization — a group of assorted young people loosely gathered together on a basis of good intentions toward some vaguely Catholic purpose. Not even the Gallic genius for drawing diagrams has been able to put the membership methods and aims of J.I.C. into a pictorial syllogism. Any time a French organization cannot do that, you may be certain it was born dead. The primary cause of J.I.C.'s nebulosity is the definition of its membership. It is an organization formed to meet the needs of young people who are neither workers nor students. At first glance that sounds as if the "I" should stand for "idle." But the French word "ouvrier" smells of dirty hands and overalls. Once a French Canadian can work with his coat on, even as a bank clerk at ten dollars a week, he likes to consider himself out of that class. He then goes into J.I.C. along with university graduates who are starting off in their professions. How do you plan a program to suit the boy with two years of high school and the college graduate?

Apart from this, J.I.C. is dealing with the most notoriously hard to organize class, the white-collar worker. As this group continues to solidify in such things as newspaper guilds and teachers' unions, J.I.C.'s work may become more effective. It should be noted here that, of its nature, J.I.C. cannot be judged entirely by its group accomplishments but rather by the influence exerted by its members in their local-professional fields. It is not easy to put such results into statistics.

However, alongside J.O.C., J.I.C. is a comparative failure and from this we may draw two conclusions. Young people do not flock to a Jocist-type organization simply because they are French, and the homogeneity of conditions and aims among "La Classe Ouvriere" affords an especially fertile field for this sort of lay apostolate.

THE J.E.C.

J.E.C., the student youth movement, is much more successful than J.I.C. as an organization, much less influential than J.O.C. as a molder of environment. The reasons for this are obvious. Compared to J.I.C., J.E.C. has the advantage of homogeneous membership. Unlike J.O.C., it works in an environment, Catholic schools conducted largely by priests and religious, already molded. Its main functions are then the promotion of leisure-time activities, in which field it is very active, and the encouragement of self-effort by the student. For the most part, it merely reinforces the lessons taught in school.

In practice, as seen in its publications and through the activities at its Centrale, J.E.C. tends to be undergraduate in a very enthusiastically intellectual way. It is Cultural with a capital "C." It knows the World's Great Symphonies by heart, can jump to its feet at the first note of the orchestra, take the beat from Bruno Walter and guide the gramophone through four full movements, stopping for appreciative gasps at the proper places. It reads Claudel and understands every word of the Satin Slipper. It stages Gheon and boos burlesque shows out of town.

It is cultural with a small "c." it knows the roots from which it springs, learns from the books and city instructors the real old French Canadian songs and dances (and is thoroughly disgusted with the real old French Canadians who sing modern songs and dance modern dances). It spins and weaves and carves in wood. It forms societies to preserve the purity of the French language and deeply resents the Americanization of its beloved Old Quebec.

These activities give Quebec university life a much greater resemblance to the Latin Quarter than to any American campus. (The University of Montreal calls its student publication *Le Quartier Latin*; J.E.C.'s paper for colleges and high schools is called *La Vie Etudiante* and its organ for the lower grades — read by three out of every four students — is named *Francois.*) They also reveal the two-fold self-consciousness of the French mind. Living in what is, after all, a geographically isolated corner of Latin America, he is conscious of himself as Catholic in a Protestant milieu, as French in an English-dominated economy. These two minority feelings tend to mingle and find release in a religious-racial apostolate in which it is often hard for the outsider to discern whether Catholicism or French Canadianism is the dominating factor. It is to the credit of the French Canadian's integrity that he cannot see any distinction between the two.

J.E.C., then, is made up, and charged with molding thought among, the future leaders of a people which clings tenaciously to its past in order to preserve its individuality and prevent absorption into the flattened masses of Anglo-American civilization. Hence the interest in Art and in arts. It is consciously cultural because it wants to prove that it is better than the rest of North America.

Self-conscious effort in such directions has its less pleasant aspect. It can foster a narrow nationalism by making good grow only in its own backyard and it can build up that frame of mind which led a German writer to write a book entitled, *Le Bon Dieu, est-il Francais?* Against these things J.E.C. must fight, while cherishing the tradition which breeds them. The fight is complicated by the fact that the two oppressed minority feelings have resulted in the setting up of two mutually contradictory goals. On the one hand, young French Canada wants to make over materialistic North America in the image of Christ, on the other hand it would like to dethrone its economic overloads and become itself a leader in that very industrial civilization against which its Catholic face is set.

When J. E. C. attempts to solve these problems, it is faced with a rock-bottom test of sincerity and courage in the lay apostolate. It must influence youth to see beyond political, social, economic and artistic aims to the single end of integrated Christian living. It must subordinate deep-rooted, and in themselves legitimate, national aspiration to basic Catholic ideals.

Even with the great good will and able Catholic lay leadership which does exist in J. E. C. (its best people are the very cream of the lay apostolate), it is still not possible to say that this has been done.

It would take a much longer and more detailed discussion than this over-simplification of the Jecist picture to give a fair estimate of J. E. C. success and failure. Let it be sufficient to say that when we ask ourselves the question "Is the Jecist's milieu as much more fundamentally Christian because of J. E. C. as the Jocist's is because of J.O.C.", we must answer that it is not.

ANOTHER OBSTACLE

This points to another obstacle to the application of the Jocist method outside the milieu for which it was developed: the difficulty of setting up, and working out the practical application of, a set of basic Christian objectives toward which the organized effort of individual apostles can be directed.

This difficulty, the J. I. C. problem of heterogeneous membership, and the tendency to cut every cloth exactly to the J.O.C. pattern are the chief, perhaps the only, barriers against applying the J.O.C. technique to any form of Catholic Action anywhere.

To overcome them, we must start with individuals rather than with an organization. These individuals must be steeped in a basic philosophy of integral Catholic living, must be able to select immediate objectives for the application of that philosophy and then must influence other individuals toward the attainment of the ends set. These immediate objectives will fall into natural groupings and from the divergence of these groups of ends will arise separate organizations for the coordination of effort.

One final important note. The Canadian Jocists retain an atmosphere of freedom, of real lay effort, of individuality, of naturalness, and at the same time adhere very strictly to the definition of Catholic Action as "the participation of the laity in the work of hierarchy." Like every Catholic Action organization it works under the bishop's mandate. Without that mandate it is not part of Catholic Action. They are very strict about that up here. When Father Lord, for example, brings his six-day summer school to Montreal, he is not allowed to call it by its thirteen-year-old-name, The Summer School of Catholic Action. The Sodality is not Catholic Action.

In doing this, the Jocists set us another fine example of genuinely Catholic Lay Apostolate and teach us that Catholic militants, like any soldiers, can only win wars by obeying orders. A rather important lesson.

JIM SHAW
Montreal
October, 1946.

For those who are not certain:
    Catholic Action has nothing at all
    To do with playing basketball.

The Catholic Worker

LONG BEFORE POPE PIUS XI ISSUED HIS call for the participation of the laity in the work of the hierarchy (Catholic Action), Peter Maurin, a French peasant, went about "doing good." Born in Languedoc, a province in the southern part of France, almost seventy years ago, Peter was educated in the village school, studied in Paris, taught at the Christian Brothers' school in Paris, came to Canada, then the United States, worked at manual labor, lived with the poor, and, by the personal practice of the works of mercy, indoctrinated them, taught them, as they doubtless taught him. His mother died when he was nine and his father married again; altogether there were twenty-three children in the family. There were too many for one small plot of land to take care of, so most of them spread out over the world. Many became teachers — sisters and Christian Brothers. The only member of his family with whom he was in touch before the war was a brother who was the head of a boys' school in Paris. Peter's real name is Aristede Pierre Maurin, and he Americanized his name as so many do, calling himself Peter Maurin (pronounced Morrin). Too many, he said, pronounce his name as though he were an Irishman.

One of the best articles written about Peter is one called "Apostle on the Bum," by Joseph Breig, published by *The Commonweal* some years ago. I tried to write a book about Peter (not a biography), but it was hard work and it has been turned down by two publishers. So I have given up trying to peddle it, though we could use the royalties.

INTEGRITY: November, 1946

It was hard to write, because it is hard to write about one whom one considers a saint without being fatuous. In a review last Sunday in the *New York Times* of "Joy," Bernanos' latest book, the reviewer states how hard a job it is to write about a saint. Another writer once pointed out that in writing about Christlike men one author turned his character into a *Don Quixote* and another into an *idiot*. It is not that we do not see Peter's faults. St. John of the Cross once wrote that if we look to people for leadership, the devil soon leads us to see their faults. Many people have complained of Peter's extremism, his lack of judgement, his blind spots, etc., but there are few who do not concede that he is that rare thing, an integrated person, a consistent person.

HE TALKS ABOUT VOLUNTARY POVERTY, AND he leads a life of voluntary poverty and detachment to an extreme so that one can never forget his shabbiness, his lack of all goods even of cleanliness.

"I have never asked anything for myself," he said to one member of our group who was asking for twenty acres of Maryfarm when he had been offered three. And Peter takes what he is handed in the way of clothes, and if we do not see that he has blankets, he goes without, and if we do not see that he has warm underwear, he goes without; he sleeps where he is put, whether it is in a dormitory or a little private room of his own; he has no money in his pocket, has no control over any of the money in any way, either in advising or counseling. He is an enunciator of principles, he says, and it is up to us to carry them out. As for himself, he is as free as the air, as St. Francis desired his followers to be. Peter indeed "seeketh not his own."

Peter talks about a philosophy of work, and all his life he has shown his respect for manual labor by participating in those labors, as a ditch digger, a railroad worker, a lumberjack, etc. He used to live on the Boweries and the Skid Rows of the country, in the cheap lodging houses, living on coarse, cheap food, wearing coarse, cheap clothes. If anyone asks him for anything, he gives it to him, without judgement. In a long lifetime he must have been tempted many times to judge. But he has never turned people away, always sharing what he had, giving up his cloak too, when asked for his coat. He was once held up in a park in Harlem, coming from a meeting, and like St. Cantius, he tried to tell the robbers where the money was, and in return for his attempt to speak to them, they blacked his eye. "This, then, was perfect joy."

HE HAS SPOKEN AT COLLEGES, SEMINARIES, UNIversities and schools around the country. He has spoken about education, secularism, the separation of religion from life, from education, from business; he has spoken about modern industrialism, modern business organizations and corporations. He has talked of Personalism and Communitarianism. It was he who brought the Personalist Manifesto to this country and induced the monks at St. John's to translate it and Longmans Green to publish it. It was he who has done so much to popularize the writings and teachings of Eric Gill. He has written many little essays, as we call them, in his phrased writing, synopsizing the thoughts of other writers and presenting them to us. He has not claimed to be an original thinker, but he has spoken of the need for a synthesis, and he, more than any other man of his day, has presented that synthesis to the world. He has done what St. Thomas did in his day, in this making of a synthesis, and probably many will be aghast at my effrontery in making this claim for him.

To be very frank, many think I am engaging in a false humility in writing about him, because I have been so much the active member of the team of Peter Maurin and Dorothy Day. My background as journalist and radical and convert to the faith enabled me to see and to popularize Peter's ideas. I have indeed tried to work them out, and the results have been, before the war, thirty-two houses of hospitality and farms around the country where groups of people tried to express their love of God and each other by working out these ideas. The intervening war took many of our workers from us, many have married and are raising families, but the work goes on — there are eight houses still running and four farms still active, and many young couples are going to the land because of the vision that Peter has held up to them. I have learned, as St. Francis said was necessary, by doing. But the more we have worked, the more I have learned that one must *be* rather than *do*. The doing follows from the being.

THAT IS WHAT PEOPLE WHO DO NOT RECOGnize Peter's importance to this movement do not understand. It took a man of Peter's vision and integrity, a man who was the embodiment of what he talked about, to move the heart and the will to act. People respond to Peter. He has a childlike faith in people and always expects much of them. He may be disappointed often, but he continues in faith and hope.

It is because of our recognition of the necessity of being rather than doing, that we turned that farm at Easton into a retreat house for the readers of *The Catholic Worker*.

AT THESE RETREATS PRIESTS COME AND GIVE us talks on the spiritual life and, after the spiritual reading at table, we give them talks on the secular life. Reading Father Vincent McNabb and Eric Gill is a help. Because God has put men on earth to praise His Holy name we have learned to sing the Mass every day, and it is a great joy. Because Pius X said that the restoration of the social order will come about through the participation of the laity in the sacrifice of the Mass and the recitation of the Divine Office, we say Prime and Compline. We say the Angelus before meals and have reading at table. Everyone who comes to the retreats, which emphasize silence, participates in the work: the women in the breadmaking, cooking, cleaning, sewing—and this summer there was carding, teasing and cleaning of wool for spinning, knitting and weaving; the men in digging ditches, mending roads, harvesting, building, etc. We have no modern plumbing at the farm in the way of bathtubs and flush toilets, and at first our primitive outhouses and taps seem like destitution to some of our guest, even the poorest of them from the cities. Poverty, manual labor, the use of the other spiritual weapons of silence, prayer, meditation, reading, listening to conferences — all these are weapons of attack on the present iniquitous social order. We hope that those who come to us, as well as those who read the paper, will be led to examine their consciences on their work — whether or not it contributes to the evil of the world, to wars — and then to have the courage and resolution to embrace voluntary poverty and give up their jobs, lower their standard of living and raise their standard of thinking and loving.

A BRIEF HISTORY

Probably I am writing too generally. The readers of this article perhaps would like more definite information. The Catholic Worker started in 1933, in a little apartment on East Fifteenth Street (not an office, but a slum flat where I lived). Because we talked about the poor, about food, clothing and shelter, about the unemployed, they flocked to us and they wanted help. Whom do I mean by us? Peter and me, Dorothy Weston (a young college graduate), and three or four unemployed, among them Stanley Visnauskas, a young Lithuanian boy just out of school and beginning to write. (A school teacher had changed his named — for some strange reason of her own — to Vishnewski, which should almost be a whole essay on the blind and idiotic attitude to our brothers who have come from countries far away and who have brought with them, and lost, a culture far superior to the brash, materialistic, pagan culture of the Kingdom of this world.) We expanded our offices, moved families who were being evicted, found homes, picketed in strikes, and sold the paper on the streets. Orders came in from all over the world and subscriptions poured in, in bundles and single orders. At one time our circulation was up to one hundred and fifty thousand, but that was before wars begun. With the Ethiopian war, the Spanish civil war, and our insistence on the futility in this day and age of using any but non-violent techniques to oppose the evils of the world, our bundle circulation began going down and our single circulation to go up. Our present circulation is an authentic one. We mail out from fifty to fifty-two thousand copies and the rest are sold during the month or on the streets. John Curran, a disciple of Peter, both in talk and work, is now the leader in the street apostolate since Stanley has turned to the printing press on the farm.

AN ILLUSTRATION OF WHY OUR CIRCULATION WENT DOWN: Before the National Biscuit Company strike back in 1935, Cathedral High School in New York took three thousand copies of *The Catholic Worker* and let the girls pay their penny a copy. (We sell the paper for a cent a copy and twenty-five cents a year.) The girls were so enthusiastic about the paper and its policies, most of all its action, that when we picketed the Mexican Consulate, protesting the persecution of the Church in Mexico and giving comfort and public support to our suffering fellow Catholics below the border, a thousand of the girls turned out to picket with us; the harassed policemen made us walk all the way around the block each time, in an effort not to obstruct traffic. (I was arrested once for obstructing traffic when there were only sixty of us picketing. But that was when I was a radical and not a Catholic. Catholics are generally considered respectable people, God help us.) When the national Biscuit Company strike came about, we went out on the picket line to distribute our paper. One of our aims is to reach the man in the street with the social teachings of the Church, and a man is certainly in the street when he is on a picket line. Often dispossess notices follow loss of salary, or direct social action of this kind. Many a time we pamphleteers, propagandists — whatever you may choose to call us — were pushed into the picket line. Our memories are filled with amusing incidents. Once during a flurry of violence when the police were riding down the picketers (Stanley was there too, dizzy with trying to get between me and a large horse, and trying to see everything that was going on) I heard Frank O'Donnell, our circulation manager (now with a family of seven children on St. Benedict's Farm in Massachusetts), call out in dulcet tones, "Remember, my children, the doctrine of our holy founder — we are all gentle personalists" The girls of Cathedral High School enthusiastically joined us in boycotting the products of the National Biscuit Company, going to their neighborhood stores and delicatessens and telling the clerks that until the strike was settled they would buy no more of their products. The heads of the corporation took alarm, and in their rage at the loss of profits (how they suffer when you hit them in their pocketbooks) went to the heads of the school.

Whom to believe — the rich or the poor? Who is listened to, the fellow with the dinner pail or the executive, clean, respectable, who by his own efforts in this democratic country, has gotten ahead and is now worthy to sit beside the bishop at communion breakfast?

Anyway the order for three thousand papers was canceled.

Little by little our circulation went down in this way. Nevertheless we consider that we have quite a large circulation, as papers go. Sixty thousand readers are not to be sneezed at or disregarded in any other way. *The Nation* once pointed out our significance in the labor movement, and said that we were a starry-eyed little publication, unfortunately with a very small circulation. I note with joy that *Integrity*, too, has been referred to by *Time* as starry-eyed, or was it bright-eyed? We may have to be caustic at times, but God forbid that we should ever with bitterness dull the sparkle in our point of view. If we are forever trying to put on the new man and see all things as new, as St. Paul says, we will have the joy and wonder of children in our apostolate in this world, which God made good and so loved that He sent his Son into it to save it.

HOW DO WE KEEP GOING THESE FOURTEEN YEARS? Nobody takes a salary. We take our clothes and food out of the common store, we share our rooms and our floor space. So everything stretches and always we can take care of one more. Readers help with donations. They send a dollar instead of the twenty-five cents yearly subscription price. Little miracles happen. A soldier sends his pay check and it just happens to be in time to keep the light and gas from being turned off. An old lady comes and leaves a box of coins which turns out to be sixty dollars. If Mr. Briggs or Mr. Ford came in and left a donation, we would consider that we had failed in our noble vocation. Thank God for the pennies of the poor. Thank God for the priests and nuns who send in offerings and help in the lay apostolate.

That doesn't mean that we are not ambitious. Right now we should like to get a nice piece of waterfront property for a retreat house for girls, to preach the family apostolate and get them out of the factories and offices. We are praying confidently to St. Joseph, picketing St. Joseph, the homefinder, for a place on the sea where we can gather driftwood for fuel, and catch eels and dig clams for food. To me, a bit of beach is a sample of heaven, and I believe firmly with St. Catherine of Siena that all the way to heaven is heaven, because He said "I am the Way."

So that is our purpose and our aim — to make it that way for our brothers whom we love, for love of Him who came to bring us a more abundant life, beginning here and now.

DOROTHY DAY
October 1946.

The "new" Magna Charta
    Has no room for the martyr,
Poverty is looked at askance.
    We are saved from obscurity
By social security,
    As for judgment,
We'll just take a chance.

Can anything good come out of a concentration camp?

Apostles In Prison

PROCLAIMED TO OUR DEAF EARS FOR half a century by the popes, it struck us squarely between the eyes only when we settled down behind the barbed wire as guests of the Japanese. Like must convert like. "It is a great law of nature and of grace," writes Pius XII, "that similarity opens the door to rapprochement and to affection." God became MAN to save MAN. Christ became a worker to save the workers. St. Francis and Peter Maurin became poor to save the poor. Thus the Incarnation is continued.

Does not the same Incarnation demand specialized Catholic Action? "Each state of life will have its corresponding apostle: workers apostles of workers; farmers apostles of farmers; sailors apostles of sailors; students apostles of students." (Pius XI)

Thank God for Stanley Camp at Hong Kong and all He permitted to be done for Him there. There is no resurrection without a passion. I think it was Father Reinhold who said that burning churches are a splendid light by which to study Catholic doctrine. In camp we had no church or even a chapel to burn. But the very absence of this and so many other "essentials" resulted in untold blessings. God's greatest gifts are usually camouflaged. At first sight they seem repulsive but there is a pearl of great price within. Not a few have written back from England, Australia and Canada admitting they have not found anywhere else the peace they discovered the hard way among their fellow internees.

ONCE THE BATTLE OF HONG KONG WAS OVER AND the bayonets were on the one side, only then did a great development begin. But how discouraging it was for several months. A year passed before we had four small groups of promising leaders. In the early months of the camp we were some thirty priests and forty nuns giving the best that was in us. The health of many hit a new low. The attitude of the laity was: "Religion is *their* business not *ours*." And I'm afraid we sometimes gave them the impression they were better off minding their own business than taking an active part in the Church's affairs. My superior during the internment, Father B. F. Meyer (who went to China with the first group of Maryknollers in 1918), used to say, "The Catholic Church is the only army in the world in which the officers do all the work."

But later when all the nuns and all but two of the priests had left the camp in 1942 (by repatriation or by hook and crook into free China), the laity began proving their mettle. Once well organized through Father Meyer's genius, they accomplished more for God and the Church than did all of us clergy and religious in the early days of the internment.

Which is as it should be. For as Canon Cardijn said in his fiery address at the first national seminarians' study week of Catholic Action at Notre Dame last August — "The Lay Apostolate is an apostolate of its own which cannot be replaced by the priestly apostolate. It is essential to the Church. This arises not from any lack of priests in the world but from the very limitations of the priestly ministry." Even many more saintly vocations to the priesthood or religious life could not of themselves take the place of organized Catholic Action.

THOUGH WE HAD HAD SOME CONTACT WITH Jocism in theory before the war, we soon became guilty of an awful lot of hitting and missing during the early days of concentration. But nothing increases experience so much as mistakes. An apparent failure is often better than an apparent success. By the end of the school year, through sheer doggedness , the impossible had become possible, though as yet quite improbable. People were still asking, with great doubts behind the question, what will become of Catholic Action and all the groups at the end of the war? Living by faith was extremely hard at times, but it is now no longer necessary in this regard.

After the war several carried on with their cell in England, adding new blood, and are now linked up with the Young Christian Workers there. Others are working with the same YCW in Australia. Three of the girls are taking a year's course with the Grail in America to continue their preparation toward spending their lives in the lay apostolate. None, as far as I know, has decided to enter seminary or convent. But several have married other Catholic Actionists (feeling that just marrying a Catholic was no longer sufficient). We have great confidence that such homes will answer the problem of vocations for both the religious and lay apostolate.

BY THE END OF 1943 WE HAD SEVEN SPECIALIZED C.A. groups, having in no case over nine members: policemen, business men, nurses, young men, young women, and two student groups (sexes separated). Officially, there was no working class, but factually, every able-bodied person was a worker. There were no "Lords" or "Ladies" or "Sirs" but there were to the end two "Fathers." Our manual labor back at Maryknoll had left its mark. Far from losing the respect of the people, the long hours we spent in the gardens, carrying wood during the night from junk to communal kitchen,

"AM I MY BROTHER'S KEEPER?"

doing our own laundry, cooking, etc., only drew laity and clergy closer together in an understanding neither had experienced before. Clothes do not make the priest. Even in shorts and barefooted it was always "father." Sometimes I think we forget that Christ did not become a priest *after* those long years as a carpenter but *before*.

These seven groups were gradually knit together with a great bond of charity and confidence. They followed a definite ten-point program (five for their own intellectual and spiritual development and five apostolic) which they themselves helped us to formulate. It was purposely made rather stiff so as to exclude all but the most generous. Those showing signs of natural leadership, even though they were not regular at their religious duties, received especial encouragement. This was given partly by the priest but chiefly by ardent C.A. members who went far beyond their duty in frequent reception of the sacraments and lived Christian lives. *Like* must convert *like*. The layman is the apostle of the layman.

THE ONLY WAY TO BECOME A LEADER IS BY LEADing. No silent recipients were allowed in our C.A. groups. All had to give as well as receive. No new-comer could drop in at these meetings but had to go through a period of probation, working with a C.A. companion (like the disciples the cell members were sent out two by two) and coming along to the monthly joint section meeting where the reports and discussions were less confidential and were planned to have popular appeal with view to interesting and initiating others in C.A. In the cell meeting everyone took a weekly assignment and reported on it the following week. Besides these action and contact assignments which were always directly or indirectly apostolic, there were four regular formative assignments the members took upon themselves in turn: 1) To prepare the study topic for the next meeting (e.g. we had four meetings on each sacrament with its social implications and relation to the Mystical Body; 2) To discuss the coming week's liturgy and make an application of one of the gospels to the group; 3) To share with the group some thought from one's spiritual reading or meditation during the week; and 4) To give a short report on the previous Sunday's sermon and apply it to the specific group. (We priests learned plenty about ourselves in this little discussion.)

Two principles we ever strove to drive home:
1) You cannot *give* what you have not *got*; and
2) You cannot *keep* what you do not *share*.

The first principle demands self development before one dare hope to have a good influence on others. The second reminds us that God has never given us anything for ourselves alone, but has always given it to be shared with other members of the Mystical Body. If we do not share it we lose it. England had ceased to share her Catholic Faith with other nations and had ceased to be mission-minded before the Reformation. We know the result. So with other nations. So too with individuals. But our Faith is of such a nature — like the loaves and fishes — that the more we share it with others, the more we teach it to others, the more we have left for ourselves.

THE EVENING ROLL-CALL IN THE CAMP WAS AT six o'clock, after which there could be gatherings within the respective blocks but no passing between blocks. For a long period the endless evenings were mostly wasted and complained against. Father Meyer, always adapting himself to circumstances, started, with the help of a couple of loyal C.A. members, a central study club of ten professional men, two from each of the five blocks in the camp. Most of these were non-Catholic and the text chosen for study was Aldous Huxley's *Ends and Means.* The discussions were most provocative and lent themselves to much positive explanation of Catholic social doctrine. Then two by two these men went back to their own block and at a convenient time after rollcall conducted a weekly open forum on the matter discussed at the central club. Every block contained C.A. members, men and women, who made it a point to attend the forums and take part in the discussions. Much constructive thinking was done as a result of these meetings and the public opinion of the camp was greatly affected. For example, several of the camp doctors felt that no children should be born in such circumstances, and had already procured a number of abortions. They emphasized the lack of food, the danger to the mother's health or even life, and the supposed injustice toward all internees who were already hungry as it was. To overbalance this growing evil, facts and principles were published widely: the Japanese gave a full adult ration for every new mouth; the mothers did suffer but camp born children were more rugged and healthy than the rest of the internees. The conclusion of one discussion was: "Perhaps our food will stop, perhaps not; so let the mothers be delivered and we will wait and see. If the rations stop a few months after birth or a few years, we then propose to kill the little ones." Sarcastic logic also helps to provoke common sense.

CATHOLIC ACTION WAS ALSO THE DYNAMIC spiritual leaven (therefore making no noise and as such staying out of the limelight) in our Catholic Youth Dramatic Society, which wrote and produced much of the amateur entertainment for the camp stage. C.A. members were the counselors for the six youth clubs, taught First Communion and Confirmation groups, kept up a regular visitation of families, especially the large families over which there was only one parent. The young ladies organized a group to visit pregnant mothers, discover their needs, and go on begging tours to collect scraps of clothing suitable for making the many little articles an infant needs. The young men and boys organized a service that produced over four hundred Christmas toys for Catholics and non-Catholics alike. Many floor boards and door frames went into these efforts, but far more went to the fireplaces to cook food. Our nurses, five Catholics among some seventy, though a bit resentful in the beginning when I suggested they could be doing more for the Church, turned out to be our hands and feet and eyes and ears in the hospital. They sometimes did for the dying what even a priest could not do, and more often prepared the way ever so delicately for the priest.

OUR IDEAL WAS TO SEE EVERY CATHOLIC MEETing together with other Catholics once a week as well as at Sunday Mass. We never reached it but came fairly close with the youth, and, of course, one hundred per cent with the children. "Pray together, work together" was a watchword. Catholicism to most people means only praying together. Our religion has become only *devotional* for Sunday morning (or other mornings if the individual is very devoted) but not a *social* reality for the rest of the day and week. So far from merely enjoying their own company at their own meetings, the Catholic Actionists planned the difficult task of bringing the other Catholics together in adult study clubs and for entertainment. A dozen more groups gradually came into being, with us priests having very little to do with them except by way of encouragement. Even the C. A. members were taught to withdraw when other talent had been found or developed sufficiently to take over. CATHOLIC ACTION IS NOT POLITICAL ACTION. It strives constantly to pass on responsibility to others. "Don't help others to help *themselves*," we used to say, "but help others to help *others*." The original leaven does not go to the ends of the mass, but permeates only what immediately surrounds it. This in turn does the same for that which is closest to it, "until the whole is leavened."

THE VITAL SOURCE OF THIS DEEP TRANSFORMATION WAS THE MASS. We gave a series of sermons on the Holy Sacrifice during the early months, with little effect. But six months after introducing the Dialogue Mass in English, when the various groups were asked what they would like to study, the answer was invariably "the Mass." There is one way to learn something and that is by doing it. And when the laity began "doing" the Mass, they began knowing it and loving it—and, incidentally, the priest began loving it much more too. The Dialogue Mass was the occasion of two very helpful ideas: a small offertory procession was instituted, and a two-minute meditation on some thought from the day's liturgy was given before each Mass. Two men representing the congregation carried up the wine (camp-made from raisins) and whole wheat altar breads. Most internees had plenty of sufferings and heartaches so the symbolism of these poor offerings was not lost. There were no offertory collections (nor Mass stipends), another apparent curse we soon realized was a blessing. The daily thought from the liturgy was a stimulation to both priest and people, and a splendid opportunity to apply the Mass to our daily Calvary.

It was intelligent participation in the Dialogue Mass and then living this in Catholic Action that developed many intimate and lasting friendships which became more intimate and more lasting because so unselfish. All the world loves a lover, but also a true lover loves all the world; yes, even one's enemies — even one's country's enemies artificially made one's own. So various C. A. groups initiated a little "Love Your Enemies Campaign." This was based on the conviction that only a part of the truth about the Japanese had been published (the worst part, of course), in England and America, in order to whip up hatred and keep feeding that monster called war. An inquiry was made. The results were most impressive. Almost every young person (it was too much to expect of most older people who had lost everything, including a sense of balance) had witnessed at least an act or two of Japanese kindness and generosity. Some brought eight or ten charitable incidents. On the other hand, hardly five per cent had actually witnessed an atrocity. These brutalities had been broadcast from the house tops, while the many acts of humaneness were not mentioned. It was inquiries like these that resulted in two more groups: one studying the Pope's Peace Points, the other studying Christian Pacifism under the title *Beati Pacifici*. Gregg's *The Power of Nonviolence* helped us immensely.

IT WAS INQUIRIES ALSO LIKE THESE THAT caused me to remain in the camp after VJ day when the British, Dutch, Norwegians, Belgians, etc. went free and the Japanese, Formosans and Koreans were interned. There is no obstacle to Catholic Action. While Father Meyer went into Hong Kong proper to begin a club for service men (with as many as seventeen hundred patrons a day) and started meetings with small groups of them, out at Stanley I found myself the chaplain of the Chinese Carmelites, of the prison with its three hundred and fifty war criminals (war heroes if the tide had changed) and four internment camps comprising in all about thirteen thousand souls. I speak no Japanese, nor Formosan, nor Korean. But many in the prison and camps spoke English and there were a couple of Catholics among them. A discussion-instruction group was started. A young Korean Dominican, Father Ri, was ordained just at this time in Macao. Father Ri had made most of his studies in Japan. He had no sooner requested it than his superiors sent him to Stanley (where he still is doing wonderful work in the prison but hopes soon to be going to Japan where the several thousands of Japanese internees have since been repatriated). Father Ri is "sold" on the lay apostolate. Our other addition was a young Chinese, Father Liu, who was also wide open to "new methods of apostolate." He was able to speak to the Formosans and the many Chinese women who had married Japanese and freely chose to be interned with them. Small groups in three languages were started in each of the camps. The British authorities cooperated most generously. By January, 1946 we had well over four hundred, mostly Japanese, under instruction. The new contacts were always made by laymen who were also gradually being made to feel responsible for following up on them.

THERE IS NO OBSTACLE TO CATHOLIC ACTION. Or, as it was expressed as far back as Pius X by His Holiness: "In any class of people whatever, chosen ones can always be found and formed." It was the same Holy Father that said near the beginning of this century: "What is most necessary at the present time to save society is to have in each parish group of laymen at the same time virtuous, enlightened, determined and really apostolic." Why, in God's name, did we have to wait for two world wars and four years in concentration behind the barbed wire before we could see it his way? I am beginning to suspect we had more mental and spiritual freedom in camp than many had back here in industrialized, regimented America. Yes, something good has come out of concentration, but God forbid that we ask for the whole hellish mess all over again in order to discover the truth which Pius XII is still preaching to our deaf world: Catholic Action is *"the great undertaking which above all others we take to heart for the supreme good of all souls and of all nations."*

DONALD L. HESSLER, M.M
Maryknoll
September 1946

The Leaven

HOW TO RECONVERT A POST-CHRISTIAN western world to Catholicism? This seems to be the most important question in the Church, to which all other problems are related. Where is there mission territory so distant as not to be subject to influences arising in Europe and America? Our political quarrels, our wars, our radios, our denatured food, our second-rate movies, our pornographic magazines, the split in Christendom which is the Protestant heresy, our immodest dress, our culture, such as it is; all reach to the far corners of the world. How can we hope that orientals or African Negroes will carry on if we fail? We are obviously bent on dragging the whole world with us to destruction. Whether we like it or not, we have to attack the very difficult problem of self-reform, for it seems that in us circumstances have placed the present hope of the world.

We must see the United States as missionary territory. There is a revival of apostolic spirit (which is a measure of the health of the Faith) going on. It is evident, for instance, in the over-crowded notitiates of Maryknoll. What is late in arriving is an intensely apostolic spirit on the home territory, an earnest hope for the soul of the girl at the next desk or the local politician.

If our problem were to introduce Christianity into some new planet recently discovered, we could proceed on simple lines. The Church has a pattern for this sort of apostolic work: a pattern of the formal presentation of the Good News, and of nasty, but fruitful, martyrdoms. What we now need is a pattern for the reconversion of a once-Christian society which thinks the Good News old stuff, and wherein the Christians themselves have absorbed large amounts of their pagan environment.

To date there has been just one really revolutionary technique offered for making this type of conquest; a technique which is adequate to the circumstances, which has had some startling successes, and which represents a flowering in experience and practice of the doctrine of the Mystical Body. This is Specialized Catholic Action. It is new, and little understood, in the United States. Many people are trying to learn the techniques, but few are able to see the woods for the trees. This article will attempt to explain major Catholic Action methods, not in detail, but as they relate to the problems at hand.

THE IDEA OF THE LEAVEN

Specialization is the one absolutely basic and essential characteristic of Catholic Action.[1] It is the idea of like by like. The once-Christian world is to be reconverted from within by simultaneous apostolic effort in every stratum of society, every professional, vocational, age or other distinctive group, by the Catholics who do already find themselves there.

---

[1] Catholic Action never really operates except under bishop's mandate. That is why Catholic Action is defined as "the participation of the laity in the apostolate of the Church's hierarchy."

This article omits discussion of the relationship of Catholic Action and the hierarchy of the Church. The necessity of subordination to the hierarchy stems not from the nature of Catholic Action, which we are here discussing, but from the nature of the Church. Every form of public apostolate must be exercised under the "hierarchy of jurisdiction." Catholic Action has also a special dependence, as being auxiliary and official; publicly proclaimed so by Pius XI.

The Leaven

Gathering spiritual strength from the Eucharist, Catholics are to be as yeast in the dough of society, acting as a leaven to raise society to God. The font of strength, which is grace, will be the same for all; as will the ultimate objective, the salvation of souls. The means will vary according to circumstances, but each Christian will be an apostle to his own kind. Doctors will be apostles to fellow doctors; clerks to other clerks; laborers to fellow laborers, intellectuals to intellectuals.

There may not, at first glance, seem to be anything very revolutionary about the idea of specialization. But consider how it cuts across most of our present concepts and methods.

An ingrained prejudice that must go is that of patronization, the idea of the salvation of the lower classes by the upper, of the ungifted by the gifted. There is a certain reciprocity of gifts owing in the nature of society, a necessary trading of talents. But it does not need to extend between classes and groups in the matter of the salvation of souls. The rich owe their superabundant wealth to the poor; but one poor man will do better in converting his neighbor to Christ than will the rich man who doesn't "speak their language." Intellectuals have a certain, not unimportant function to perform in society. But in the matter of turning men again to God, let the intellectuals persuade their fellow intellectuals rather than make plans for the conversion of the laboring masses, who are (as the Jocists have proved) capable of effecting their own resurrection. These two classes represent the two great apostasies of recent centuries. The intellectuals will do their greatest good turn for the workers by converting fellow intellectuals, and so stopping the stream of atheistic and pornographic matter now channelled in the direction of the laboring classes.

AMERICANS MAY OBJECT THAT SPECIALIZATION will have the effect of formalizing class and other distinctions between peoples, and so be "anti-democratic." But distinctions are good so long as they represent a wholesome diversity among people. The universality of Catholicism can unite on a higher level people with differences of national customs, of temperament, of intellectual power and of income. It is safer for most people's salvation that they live within a traditional pattern, so long only as it is good. When we are all saints we can mingle freely without envy or covetousness.

Preserving distinctions, however, does not mean preserving unhealthy ones. There will be a lot of individual readjustment going on because of the present disorder in society. Catholic Action ought to help, this by stimulating intellectual and spiritual life. When we see worldly young men turning to the priesthood, Hollywoodish glamour girls discovering that they are really not ashamed of their immigrant parents and "foreign" neighborhood; when we see the "get-ahead" boys practicing voluntary poverty, college graduates choosing manual labor, and manual laborers taking to the study of St. Thomas; then we will know that society is struggling toward form and order. Each will find his own functional place in order to work there for the apostolate.

Specialization will check another unfortunate tendency here. After society has broken down very far (as now) it can only be saved by a universal improvement in morality. We often urge, instead, a system of undue checks and balances to try to prevent, by legislation or pressure groups, the growing indifference to the common good. Rather than hope for more integrity among doctors, we begin to think it might be well to put undue checks on doctors to insure their maintaining professional standards. We even (Heaven help us!)

think patients might form pressure groups to protect themselves against malpractice. And socialized medicine (which is the same tendency in its most acute form) hangs over our heads. Yet obviously what is needed is a reform of the medical profession by medics.

Similarly, we despair of virtue among tradesmen, and place our hope now in legislation against them, now in consumer pressure groups (some cooperatives amount to as much as this). Yet the grocery business, or the drug business, should be reformed by grocers or druggists, through whatever associations are suitable, and certainly accompanied by the widespread diminution of avarice and an increase in moral responsibility.

STAY IN THE DOUGH

Inherent in the idea of specialization is the corollary that the yeast must stay in the dough. From without it cannot leaven. Catholic Action is action from within; not a going out into the desert, not a leaving of society. From this follows the very firm conviction of Catholic Action adherents that it is not for the Church today to leave the rottenness of western society but to transform it. They are opposed to all of what they would call "escapist" movements; all efforts at flight away from our sick brethren into a cleaner atmosphere.

Some internal controversies in Catholic Action rage around this point. The subject is far too difficult to treat here; we shall at another time. However, several things everyone would agree on are:

1) That no Christian can in good conscience flee the problems of the day in order to save himself. If he goes away (to the land for instance), it must be for a purpose related to the salvation of his city brethren.

2) Staying in society doesn't mean approving it. A figure sometimes used is that of goldfish in a bowl of dirty water. We are not to take the fish out, but to change the water. So staying in the mess means changing it, and the real quarrels arise over how drastic a change is necessary.

3) There are two directions of action. One is the personal stimulation of one's neighbor to a deeper spiritual level (or to a state of grace), which will make reform of society possible. Without good men you cannot have a good society. The other direction is the reformation of the institutions of society, in order to make it easier for men to save their souls. The two actions develop progressively the one encouraging the other. It is in the matter of the second that there is a difference of opinion about the direction which it should take. As an obvious example of the problem, what sort of an economic order shall we work toward? One day *Integrity* will thrash out these matters.

THE CELL TECHNIQUE

Besides the all-important specialization, there are certain Catholic Action techniques which, if not always absolutely essential, are generally considered integral to the movement. The three most important are Cell Organization, Inquiry Method, and Services (or Campaigns).

The cell is mere common sense. In its essence it is organized cooperation. It is in the nature of the organism, which is the Mystical Body, for its parts to cohere. If we want to work as Christians in the apostolate, it is imperative that we work together. The most efficient way to work is in small, effective units.

Isolated individuals cannot renew our highly centralized and very pagan society. They must unite to give society form, unite to increase their influence, unite to strengthen their own faith. This should be clear to everyone by now. Even an especially gifted doctor, whose personal influence is enormous, cannot do effective work in the apostolate without some organization with his fellow Catholic doctors. The good a single doctor can do is largely a matter of personal good in particular cases. The need today goes beyond this. Medical ethics are themselves in danger of turning completely against Christian practice. It is not enough for a doctor to observe the Church's medical laws himself. If he is to save the medical profession, he must work with a guild of doctors or with a Catholic group within the American Medical Association toward a reform of medicine by doctors. The example of doctors is particularly apt because we lack in the United States any effective Catholic influence in the medical profession, despite there having been great Catholic doctors of tremendous personal, and Catholic influence within a secular framework. The late Dr. James Joseph Walsh is an example in point. Admired and respected by Catholics and non-Catholics alike, his excellent Christian ideas about medicine are already nearly forgotten, for lack of a body of doctors to perpetuate and add to them.

THERE ARE A FEW INSTANCES IN WHICH THE cell technique might prove a hindrance rather than a help. Writing, for instance, is a solitary profession which does not ordinarily lend itself to group effort. A Catholic writer would not get far without keeping in close personal touch with the lay apostolic movement, but he is hard to organize and it seems on the whole inadvisable to organize him.

The cell need not be too formalized for certain highly educated groups, but it should be compact, small (not more than a dozen members at the most), disciplined and meet regularly and frequently. It is the basic operational unit of Catholic Action. Cells should multiply rapidly once Catholic Action gets under way, there being no limit to their potential number.

Anyone who doubts the wisdom of the cell technique should consider the alternatives. Especially in the large worker and student groups, the tendency of modern society is to deal with unindividuated masses. This is a dangerous procedure. It is quite possible to sway masses of men and women by appealing to their passions; no one has yet found them particularly responsive to reason. Even relatively small, homogeneous groups of two and three hundred do not lend themselves so much to formation as to obedience. Perhaps it is the temper of the time. We certainly see it in colleges today, where students are turned out as though by rubber stamp. Thinking comes hard and the small group with everyone a responsible member seems to be the necessary condition of breaking up our irresponsibility.

THE INQUIRY METHOD

The Inquiry Method, which forms the bulk of a cell meeting, and is the Catholic Action method of procedure, is again a technique which can exceptionally be dispensed with as to formal use. However, it too is rooted in the nature of things. SEE, JUDGE and ACT, its three parts, follow the normal process of reasoning. Lawyers, or college presidents, might telescope or elaborate the steps, but without eliminating them. SEE could take the form of a nationwide, sociological survey, JUDGE represent ten years of theological study, and ACT be the formulation of national legislative policy over a period of years. It still amounts to the same thing in essence, as one-meeting inquiry on classroom cheating.

The best way to get a simple view of the Inquiry (so often made stilted and complex by the slavish following of a misunderstood formula) is to contrast it with an alternative method of mental training, the sermon, whether as heard in church or in a sodality meeting. The sermon could easily be more wise and penetrating in content than are the apostles' own inquiry findings, yet fail to move them. To make *them* think, as contrasted with making them enthusiastic about someone else's ideas, is the purpose and accomplishment of the Inquiry. In the end you really do get people who can think; people who are responsible; people who have formed Catholic minds; people in whom the Church can well hope. But the effort has to be there.

One way or another (usually through study days) it is the priest-director of a Catholic Action cell who guarantees the JUDGE material the Christian standard in the matter. The other two parts belong to the lay members, and it is from them that the priest learns the actual condition of the world from which he is largely shut off today by secularism.

The making of inquiries is not so difficult as is sometimes thought. When Catholic Action is highly organized there will probably be need for simultaneously study and action on major problems throughout the country. Then the inquiry might be centrally made and adapted locally to each milieu. In the beginnings, however, the inquiries should be made locally, and should concern problems which are immediately at hand for the cell in question.

There is a point (which is not the beginning) at which the making of inquiries becomes difficult. Obviously, the direction of Catholic Action will be determined by the subjects of the inquiries. How long should students inquire into campus morality and communal life before asking whether or not they are really getting an education? How long should clerical workers in an advertising agency work on problems of office morality and procedure before querying the morality of modern advertising? This is not subject for the present discussion, but it is important. Technique, however excellent, is merely technique. A philosophy will have to develop along with it if the resultant action is to be fruitful.

SERVICES

Services are organizations or functions which develop, on a more or less permanent basis, to solve the problems studied in the inquiries. When the problem can be solved by a one-time effort, campaigns are used. Catholic Action cells go on making more inquiries and do not themselves grow into services, but as the movement progresses it is constantly enriched by these auxiliaries which are, second only to the quality of the Catholic Action leaders themselves, the true measure of the movement's effectiveness. What might constitute a service? A credit union, a weekly folk dance, a newspaper, a magazine, a system of rehabilitating juvenile delinquents, a summer camp, a marriage preparation course, anything. The collective power of the members to finance and staff such services becomes tremendous. Herein lies the great power of Catholic Action to change the social order. Unlike mere political power, it is dynamic because it is the organic expression of a body of formed Christians. Catholic Action has the potential power to settle thousands of families on the land, should it seem wise to do so. It has the potential power to control the direction of industry, when it decides what is to be the proper direction.

CATHOLIC ACTION IN THE UNITED STATES

Beginnings of the Catholic Action can be found in nearly every center of consequence in the United States. There are cells operating, or in the formative stages, in New York, Chicago, Boston, Rochester, San Francisco, San Antonio, Detroit, Woonsocket, South Bend, and dozens of other places. The movement has begun, or is beginning, in high schools, colleges, parishes, offices, factories, among girls, boys, married women and professional men. Nearly all the groups are feeling their way, training leaders and trying out methods. Very few are officially operating under bishop's mandate. There is communication between cells in different cities, but no coordinated action so far, and not a little disagreement about the true nature of Catholic Action and the philosophy which is to accompany it.

Corporate study of Catholic Action techniques on the part of interested priests is a little further advanced. An annual study week for priests takes place in Chicago, and a priests' bulletin is regularly published from that city.

Seminarians were slower getting started in their interest, but it is increasing fast. The first seminarians' study week was held at Notre Dame this past summer.

CANON CARDIJN'S VISIT

The founder of Jocism is Canon Cardijn. His was the genius which developed Catholic Action techniques out of compassion for the masses of workers lost to the Church. Canon Cardijn is a dynamic and saintly Flemish-Belgian priest who has suffered at German hands now in two wars. He admits he feels his sixty-some years, yet can summon vitality sufficient to exhaust companions half his age. Last summer he made a whirlwind trip up and down and across

North, Central and South America, chiefly to prepare a first hand report on the lay apostolate for the Holy Father. During the trip he spoke to Catholic Action laity and interested priests in various parts of the United States. Since he is not only the supreme authority on Catholic Action but also the embodiment of its spirit, his visit had an enormous effect, both in setting our embryonic movement on correct paths and in encouraging first beginnings.

The Canon made some interesting and emphatic observations. For one thing he kept deploring the dearth of young men in the movement. This has long been a subject of regret anyhow. It has seemed that on the whole girls were more zealous and apostolic than boys and that, however desirable it might be to have masculine leadership in the abstract, in the concrete it looked as though women were going to take the initiative in restoring all things in Christ. Canon Cardijn thinks it is impossible for the movement to succeed on that basis, since he places his greatest hope in a whole generation of new and Christian families. And how can you have really Christian families if only the girls are formed Christians? Indeed it is not a new problem. Yet some would not agree with Canon Cardijn. Perhaps, they say, it is for the women to remake American men in our day, even if this is contrary to the normal order. Another case of God using the weak things of the world. Anyhow, now that the war is over, male leaders may be forthcoming.

ANOTHER INSISTENCE OF CANON CARDIJN IS on getting the movement rooted in industry. So far Catholic Action is confined largely to white collar workers and students, and not to the laboring man. One difficulty here is that boys do not go into industry at the early age that they go into it abroad. At the time which is psychologically best for attracting them to a Catholic Action movement, they are still in school. School is not a particularly good setting for Catholic Action because the problems there are not sufficiently vital. Almost the only industrial beginnings of Catholic Action so far have been among the workers of French descent in New England, where the inspiration of French Canada prevails. It cannot be said to be a typically American effort.

Most interesting of all was the Canon's insistence on the importance of the United States in the North American movement. Since Catholic Action is highly organized and effective in Canada to the north of us, in Mexico and some other Latin American countries to the south of us, why should we, in our fumbling, be the hope of the movement? Yet Father Villeneuve of Montreal, who accompanied the Canon, held to the same thesis. The Canadian Jocists, he said, have St. John the Baptist as their patron saint. Like the Precursor, they consider themselves the presages of a much greater movement in the United States, to which they would willingly be subsidiary.

If we are to be the American leaders of Catholic Action, it is certainly not because we have so far deserved it. It must be, as in political affairs, because of our natural, industrial and technical wealth and power which we can use for good or for evil. Hollywood movies too tenth-rate to make the grade in the United States, serve to degrade the peoples of many a Latin American country. Our worst pulp magazines, our cheapest clothes, our most primitive and erotic jazz music, are all passed on to the south, where political instability usually allows entry. In Quebec to the north, the Church is powerful enough still to hold the dam against a flood of our sexy advertisements and extremes of women's dresses, but for how long? If we could clean up the source of evil, our neighbors would have a much better chance of Christianizing their own lands.

Canon Cardijn always sees Catholic Action as a world movement. In his opinion only a world movement is sufficiently powerful and universal to overcome Communism. He foresees an international organization even before the movement is highly organized nationally. And, indeed, there is that sense of international unity already in Catholic Action. Two Chicago girls attended an international congress in Paris last summer. The New York Catholic Action cell's guest apartment is quite accustomed to visitors who do not speak English. There is a free exchange of literature from various countries, and many a cell member regrets not having studied French more assiduously in high school.

WARNINGS

Specialized Catholic Action, as we hope this article has made clear, allows for considerable adaptation according to circumstance. While using the major techniques, the movement ought normally to develop differently for each country. How it will develop in the United States is still problematical, but it ought not to be formed into a European mold. Americans ought to study their own problems very closely and ought to distinguish and preserve what is peculiar to the American temperament, as long as it is good. The Belgians take to mass, semi-military enthusiasm and demonstrations. Perhaps that is not our temper. Once we grasp the essentials and the spirit of Jocism, we ought not to hesitate to strike out as befits our own circumstances.

On the other hand, there is a false Americanism running through the lay organizations of the Church, a bling worship of American ideals as set forth by Coco-cola advertisements and the National Association of Manufacturers. We Catholics in general have conformed so to commercial ideals that we accept a shocking and gross materialism without question. Most Catholic societies have fallen into mediocrity and ineffectiveness because of their reluctance to question these "immutable" standards. It is precisely these things which Catholic Actionists must hold up to the light of Christian judgment. Yet sometimes they identify them with the American spirit, and so fail at the start. There are cells which are reluctant even to consider as possibly un-Christian, current women's fashions, the seemingly endless pursuit of "a higher standard of living," industrialism, liberal colleges, hot swing music, dating, and large cities. They end up wanting only to change the insides of people and not society, or to improve sexual morals in disregard of the occasions of sin thereof, and in disregard of the other commandments.

RATHER SIMILAR, AND EQUALLY DISASTROUS, IS a powerful anti-intellectualism which runs through young Catholics. It may have honorable roots in a detestation of the academic aridity produced in scholars by liberal education. But thinking is itself honorable, and has never been more needed. It has been said of the Jocist leaders (laboring young men) in the suburbs of Paris before the war that they had the keenest understanding of their times and their environments of any men of their day. Contrast that with the oft-heard exclamation among Young Christian Workers here: "Thank goodness, I'm no intellectual!" There literally is no hope for Catholic Action in the United States unless the movement produces some good thinkers and has a great respect for the intelligence. The philosophy that is going along with Catholic Action, for instance, is not susceptible of solution on the emotional or intuitional level. It awaits hard thinking on everyone's part.

Catholic Action should form integrated Catholics, and this should be a prelude to a high sanctity in the midst of the world. It may well be dangerous for lay people to be overly "pious" if they are not going to be integrated. But providing their spiritual life is not on the merely devotional level and is not combined with a sort of blindness in regard to the true nature of secular society, the holier the better. A girl who does not wish to conform to pagan mores is usually shuttled off to a convent someplace, wherein it is considered decent to aspire to contemplation. But those in Catholic Action are spiritually ambitious, and rightly so. Their conquest of the world will ultimately succeed only in the measure that supernatural charity overflows in them, and in the measure that the gift of Wisdom lights their way. There are contemplatives, not infrequently, in the movement elsewhere. There must be contemplatives here. One problem is to find spiritual directors who are able and willing to help the development of the spiritual life of members.

Catholic Action, especially among workers, gives rise to a "mystique," a certain characteristic spirit which is the same everywhere. It is a spirit of conquest, of contagious confidence in their ability, through Christ's power, really to change the face of society and the course of history. The vitality of Catholic Action contrasts sharply with the despair-born enervation still pervading our secular culture. It is challenged only by the Communist mystique, which it will overcome by an ever-increasing outpouring of Charity.

PETER MICHAELS
New York City
October 1946.

INTEGRITY: November, 1946

It isn't amusing to find people using
    Quotations from Pius the Twelfth,
To justify living without ever giving
    The poor man a share of their wealth.

The Workers' Apostolate

IN THE BEGINNING THERE WAS CARDIJN. Then there was a small group of young workers in a slum suburb of Brussels. Then a growing movement of young workers, boys and girls, which spread all over Belgium, from Belgium to France, to Canada, to England, to China, to Australia, to the whole continent of Europe, to the whole continent, North and South, of America.

Now, in 1946, there are a million young workers with well-established methods, recognized by their governments in many countries as the spokesmen of their whole class, accepted by the International Labor Office as the one international body to speak for all the young workers of the world. More than that, out of it has grown a movement of adult workers which, particularly in France, bids fair by its revolutionary methods to bring Christianity, a living Christianity, to the masses. All this in just over thirty years, one of the most tumultuous periods the world has yet known, during a time when mankind has been hastening through two wars to the crossroads of history.

Little wonder that the techniques they have evolved have been adopted and adapted by the majority of movements in Catholic Action, that they have earned the encomia of Popes and the respect of the Communists, that they have been called the miracle of the twentieth century and a complete type of what the apostolate should be. In the summer of this year a gathering was held in Brussels of leaders from European countries, and eighteen countries, including ex-enemy countries, were represented there. More recently still, Canon Cardijn completed a tour of the North and South American continents, and found Jocists in every country which he visited, in Canada as well as Costa Rica, in the United States as well as in the Argentine. What is the cause of its success, that is, apart from the grace of God? One adds the latter proviso, because there can be no doubt as Pius XI said: *The finger of God is here.* It must be something as universal as the Church, which transcends national boundaries, something of which the Workers' International of Marx was but a figure or even a caricature. Its success has been universal, and Pope Pius XII has said: "Now, when a new world is rising from the ruins wrought by a pitiless war, we can only hope that the laws of Jesus Christ will triumph in every part of society, as between nations, and especially, thanks to the providential leaven of the Young Christian Workers, in the mass of the workers of Belgium *and other countries.*"

The movement has been built up by the young workers themselves, but the great architect, essentially a man given by Providence to this age, is Cardijn. Its fundamental ideas are to be found in a dialectic, or rather the synthesis issuing from a dialectic, between two terms: the divine destiny of each young worker on the one hand, and their condition of life in the modern industrial world on the other. Cardijn stated this in his speech to the International Congress of 1935 in these words:

> Three fundamental truths dominate and illuminate the problem of the working youth of the world. They inspire, explain, and guide us

towards the solution which the young Christian Workers has to give:

1) A truth of faith. The eternal and temporal destiny of each young worker in particular and of all young workers in general.

2) A truth of experience. The terrible contradiction which exists between the real condition of the young workers and this eternal and temporal destiny.

3) A truth of pastoral practice or method. The necessity of a Catholic organization of young workers with a view to the conquest of their eternal and temporal destiny.

In this brief statement is summed up the tremendous dialogue between faith and reality. The Young Christian Workers is the synthesis between thesis and antithesis, between the truth of faith, that God has created each young worker with an eternal destiny which he is to achieve through fulfilling his temporal destiny here on earth, and the mocking contradiction of reality, where we find the spiritual destiny forgotten, or denied, and social conditions which are far from providing the right atmosphere in which it can be recalled or asserted. They are three truths, three facts. They are not preconceived notions, nor the tentative conclusions of an experimental sociologist, if there be such a creature. Hence the basis of the action, methods, training, organization of the Young Christian Workers is not artificial, but springs from life, from natural life and supernatural life. They are not separated in the movement as they are not separated in life. The Jocist movement is not concerned solely with saving the souls of all young workers, nor is it concerned solely with bettering their material conditions. It is concerned with both. Cardijn continues:

> There cannot be an eternal destiny at one side of, at a distance from, a material life which bears no relation to it. A destiny cannot be disincarnate, any more than religion can be disincarnate. No — eternal destiny is incarnate in time, begun in time, develops, is achieved, is fulfilled in time, in the whole of material life, in all its aspects, in all its applications, in all its achievements: bodily, intellectual, moral, sentimental, professional, civic and social life. Eternal destiny can no more be separated from temporal destiny than religion is separate from morality. AND THE WORD WAS MADE FLESH, AND DWELT AMONG US. The eternal destiny of each human being becomes incarnate, is developed and is completed here on earth, always and everywhere. Thy kingdom come on earth as it is in heaven.

For this reason you find the Jocists of Belgium putting forward plans, which are accepted by the government, for legislation concerning the hours of work of young people, while every year they undertake a great campaign to get every young Catholic to his Easter Duties. For this reason you find the Jocists of Canada taking the lead in a "Justice for the Veteran" campaign while at the same time they read and study the Gospels in order to learn how to live and act like Christ. For this reason you find the Jocists of France successfully negotiating a law concerning vacations for young workers, with pay, while at the same time they play a large role in the liturgical revival which is forging ahead in their country. For this reason you find the Jocists of England holding public meetings on housing problems, while at the same time each one of them sees that a two minutes' silence is observed at three o'clock on Good Friday in his factory.

The countries in which it had existed longest, and in which it had grown strongest, France and Belgium, were occupied by the conquering German army. The story is still to be written of the deeds and exploits of the members of the J.O.C. in these countries both in the work of the Resistance and in keeping their movement alive. Two thirds of their headquarters in Brussels were requisitioned by the Germans; in the other third the J.O.C. housed Jews who were "on the run," it printed false identity cards and false ration books, it still organized the movement. All this under a roof which was used as a shooting range by the occupying troops. In Paris the headquarters was locked and sealed, and entry was forbidden to the national leaders. So they entered by a back door, took out all the material they needed and retired to a house in the country a little way out of Paris which was loaned to them for the purpose by Cardinal Suhard. In both countries thousands of young men were rounded up and deported as forced labor to Germany. Immediately they began to organize the J.O.C. in German factories and work-camps. Priests who were chaplains volunteered to go as workmen to factories in Germany — where they continued their work as chaplains. By the end of the war there was a vast network of Jocist cells throughout Germany among all those who were doing forced labor, a network which did Inquiries, held meetings (often in Catholic rectories, due to the heroic good will of the German pastors) and carried on their work of training and of the apostolate, under impossible conditions. Both national chaplains, Canon Cardijn and Canon Guerin, were imprisoned, but both contrived to get out to continue their work of animating the whole national movement. Two of the foundation members of the first cell in Belgium, Tonnet and Garcet, died in notorious concentration camps because of the treatment they received there.

THE MOVEMENT WAS NOT OFFICIALLY CONnected with the Resistance movement as such. But in Belgium thousands of francs in forged money and thousands of ration tickets were distributed every month to people who were in hiding; refugees were succoured; a constant grim silent battle was waged with the Gestapo. During the first World War the J.O.C. was born in the fertile brain of Canon Cardijn when he was imprisoned by the Germans for suspected espionage; during the second World War the J.O.C. came of age by the heroic feats and at times almost martyr's sufferings of its members. In France many joined and fought in the ranks of the Resistance movement; some were sent to concentration camps for being members of the J.O.C. (in particular one citation mentioned that as members of Catholic Action they were working against the interests of the Third Reich); yet others were shot. Above all, in both countries, they showed the value of their training. They were leaders, leaders possessed of the greatest quality of all — they knew that a leader must know how to serve others.

Toward the end of the Occupation period there emerged an adult organization, centered on Lyons whence had migrated half of the headquarters staff from Paris when the country was divided, an adult movement which grew from the J.O.C. and which in the opinion of many will be of much greater importance in the workers' apostolate. It is called the

People's Family Movement. The formula of the J.O.C. is: Observe — Judge — Act. See conditions as they are; judge them in the light of Christian principles; then act in order to make things — and people — more as they should be. Thus action, whether individual or group, is the outcome of an inquiry. It was decided that this was not the method which would succeed in penetrating into the great non-Christian, neo-pagan, mass of adult workers. The first thing to do was to get them to act in a Christian way. So the M.P.F. organized small cells, made up of two or three families, who would find out what works of charity or mutual assistance were of immediate and urgent necessity in their neighborhood, and then called in neighboring families (whether they were Catholic or Communist) to help them. There was ample scope for this in a country which had shortages of food, clothing and housing due to the ravages of the war, the wake left by the scourges of occupation and bombing. The formula now became: Observe — Act — Judge. The results of such action are two-fold: the immediate material benefit, and then the benefit of the gift of self, the fraternal acts of charity, preparing the ground of the soul for the seeds of supernatural charity. Moreover, the decisions are taken and the action completed by, as far as possible, groups of *families* acting together, meeting together. Families *are* the movement — the masses *are* the movement. Of course the leaders, at every level, are Catholics who meet with their chaplains, who discuss matters with him, and who receive their training from him. He keeps the leaven alive and active — but the leaven is in the paste, fermenting, acting, influencing, Christianizing.

IT IS IMPOSSIBLE TO SUMMARIZE THE GROWTH of the workers' apostolate in European countries, either in numbers or in influence. However, a few facts at random may be sufficient to illustrate the power and force of the Young Christian Workers in several countries. One of the Belgian government representatives at a recent I.L.O. meeting was the National President of the J.O.C.F. (the girls' section of the J.O.C.). In Italy, within a few months of the end of the war, cells of the G.O.C. (Italian Y.C.W.) were springing up in all the industrial areas. Recently the British government sent a Commission to Germany to study the position of youth movements there, and one of the five members was the National President of the Y.C.W. In France there are some four hundred priests whose full-time work is the J.O.C. and the M.P.F. Figures, or even isolated facts, can do little to convey the vast growth of the workers' apostolate in Europe. Like life it grows; like life it is dynamic; and in this dynamic growth lies the hope of the workers and ultimately the hope of Europe and of the world.

JOHN FITZSIMONS
University of Notre Dame
October 1946.

I fear we need more drastic means
    Than periodic Missions,
To curb the nasty habits
    Of Catholic politicians.

BOOK REVIEWS

Sanctity in a Psychological Mire

JOY
By Georges Bernanos.
Translated by Louise Varese.
New York: Pantheon Books,
1946. Price: $2.75.

Joy makes melancholy reading. It is the story of one saint and a half-dozen or so very unprepossessing sinners. The saint is always joyful, but the author's mood is that of the sinners. The depression which creeps over the reader is not conducive to full appreciation of the joys of sanctity.

Chantal de Clergerie is the heroine. She is extraordinarily pure and innocent, as we are assured over and over again in the course of the book. She is a mystic who experiences ecstasies, but who is so pure and innocent that she thinks them manifestations of an hereditary nervous disease. Even the reader is not fully reassured on this point because of the almost maddening way the author has of talking around the subject. The book would be much improved by the addition of a few simple categorical statements. Everything said concerning Chantal's extraordinary gifts goes like this:

Chantal: "The secret of my . . ."
Anyone else: "Because of your . . ."

Joy would make a dull play but would be inexpensive to stage. Only three sets are necessary: the library, kitchen and Chantal's bedroom of Monsieur de Clergerie's country estate. Then a handful of actors, and almost no props. There is no action, other than an occasional walking to the door as though to leave. For the rest, interminable conversations. These are called "great dialogues which bare the secrets of souls" on the jacket blurb, but they seemed muddy to me.

In time it becomes evident that events, or rather conversations, are leading (the chauffeur keeps saying so) to a crisis of some dire sort. I couldn't discern the direction for a long time, and then I began to hope that Chantal's purity and innocence were going to save the souls of all the nasty characters; of her selfish and hypochondriac father, her avaricious, psychopathic grandmother, the miserable worm of a psychiatrist, the priest who had lost his faith and the very evil Russian chauffeur. I had especially hoped for the chauffeur, who seemed so taken with Chantal and had even foregone his daily ration of dope as a noble gesture of some sort. So the end was a rude shock and I still don't see the logic of it, but maybe that is my fault.

Joy will probably please Bernanos fans for all of that. It is not as good as his other works which have been translated but it is in the same turgid style. Bernanos must be a very unhappy man to radiate such gloom, and the wicked in Europe must be much more sickly and neurotic than the wicked here if Bernanos faithfully portrays them.

Perhaps the translator is partly responsible for the lack of clarity. Certainly it is startling to find such a heroine as Chantal exclaiming "My God," sometimes five or six times in as many pages. She probably only said "Mon Dieu," in the original.

For all that there are times when the book has power. The scene of the psychiatrist with his patient rings true, as does Chantal's charity for her grandmother.

C.J.*

---

* Presumably this book review was written by Carol Jackson. —Ed.

Book Reviews

Excellent Catholic Novel

WOMAN OF THE PHARISEES
By Francois Mauriac.
Translated by Gerard Hopkins.
New York: Henry Holt & Company, 1946.
Price: $2.50.

Pharisaism is an easy target for novelists. Besides being a fairly common failing, it has the advantage of readily winning the reader's contempt. What is rare and wonderful is a charitable presentation of a pharisaical person. Francois Mauriac has done it.

The woman, Brigitte Pian, is the second wife of a French provincial gentleman, and stepmother to his son and daughter. Pious and righteous, she habitually attributes her own meddlesome propensities to correspondence with the designs of God's Providence. She succeeds in introducing tragedy into most of the lives around her.

The story is told as the first-person reminiscences of Brigitte's step-son, supplemented by recourse to diaries and other sources. It is skillfully told, with restraint and deep spiritual insight. The characters are excellently drawn in the case of all the leading figures. But the most remarkable fact about the book is that it is an excellent Catholic novel. This is not only because it is set against a background of the Faith, but because the studies of character are really studies of souls, with the norm of sanctity always in mind. The treatment of them all is compassionate, stressing the workings of grace. A less spiritual man than the author could perceive the havoc wrought by a pious hypocrite. It takes some depth to see that no one can create havoc such that God is prevented through it from drawing souls to Him. It takes a greater depth of charity still to perceive that God loves even pious hypocrites and uses His own means to save them.

There are some beautiful spiritual passages in the book, especially in the Abbe Calou's diary and in Octavia Trombe's love letter to the indecisive Puybaraud.

P.M.*

---

* Peter Michaels? (Carol Jackson). —Ed.

EPISTLE FOR THE FEAST OF SS. JOHN FISHER AND THOMAS MORE, MARTYRS.

"IN THOSE DAYS: ELEAZAR, ONE OF THE chiefs of the scribes, a man advanced in years, and of comely countenance, was pressed to open his mouth to eat swine's flesh. But he, choosing rather a most glorious death than a hateful life, went forward voluntarily to the torment. And considering in what manner he was come to it, patiently bearing, he determined not to do any unlawful things for the love of life. But they that stood by, being moved with wicked pity, for the old friendship they had with the man, taking him aside, desired that flesh might be brought which it was lawful for him to eat, that he might make as if he had eaten, as the king had commended, of the flesh of sacrifice: that by so doing he might be delivered from death. And for the sake of their old friendship with the man they did him this courtesy. But he began to consider the dignity of his age and his ancient years and the inbred honor of his grey head and his good life and conversation from a child: and he answered without delay, according to the ordinances of the holy law made by God, saying that he would rather be sent into the other world. For it doth not become our age, said he, to dissemble: whereby many young persons might think that Eleazar, at the age of fourscore and ten years, was gone over to the life of the heathens: and so, they, through my dissimulation and for a little time of a corruptible life, should be deceived, and hereby I should bring a stain and a curse upon my old age. For though for the present time, I should be delivered from the punishments of men, yet should I not escape the hand of the Almighty, neither alive nor dead. Wherefore by departing manfully out of this life, I shall show myself worthy of my old age: and I shall leave an example of fortitude to young men, if with a ready mind and constancy I suffer an honorable death for the most venerable and most holy laws. And having spoken thus, he was forthwith carried to execution."

II MACHAB. 6, 18–28

INTEGRITY

NOWEL. To us is born our God Emmanuel!

Now-el, Now-el, Now-el. To us is

born our God Em-mān-u-el.

CONTINUED - VERSE ON REAR COVER

December, 1946  Vol. 1, No. 3

: the third issue :
SUBJECT : CHRIST WITH US

Editorial

CHRISTMAS IS ALWAYS new. It is of the gold that resists tarnish. It is a child's face recently scrubbed. It is simple, marvelously simple, charming and irresistible.

There is evident in each year's celebration of this Day the fecundity of God feeding the insatiability of man. For our having tendered the careless hospitality of the manger, the gratitude of the Infant to whom we played grudging host, is infinite.

We had at least let Him in. The shepherd and the ass were our unstudied ambassadors — these and a few foreigners who were in town that night. Someone at sometime had dug a hole or fashioned a roof (history is not sure), some sort of shelter, not much, but we let them use it for the night. For that He is infinitely grateful.

We did let Him in, and that is what counts. Being in, He is here to stay. *Deo Gratias,* He is here with us!

Name the place where He cannot be found this Christmas! In the churches, yes, but there is nothing strange in that. On that Day a lady goes about town, she seems to be everywhere, carrying a Child bundled up. Suddenly she stops wherever she happens to be and says to whomever happens to be there, "Look at my baby." The baby smiles into strange faces and the smile is the same to priest or prostitute. It answers the leer of the drunkard or the tear of the lonely.

As surprisingly gracious as the morning sun after the night of misery, is this smile of the Babe of Bethlehem.

The activity at the liquor store is tremendous, four deep around the counter, half of them jagged. A young girl chaffs nervously to be back at the party — her first office party. Three "fifths" of the Schenley's — "To Hell with the change." The glow from the neon strikes the ceiling of a room across the street, six floors up. A middle-aged woman tries to find comfort lying on her other side. The cancer, they suspect, has begun to work on the inner lining of the abdomen. Sometimes, if she lies perfectly still, she can feel just that, that sort of gnawing as if she were being eaten from the inside.

Down in the street a man sounds sick. He lurches back into the neon light and opens the door; then falls forward, his head striking the metal edge of the sill. A young fellow goes by with a Christmas tree, "The kid is three. He oughta really enjoy the show this year....."

What misery, what hunger, what despair!

The breasts of Mary are so round with milk they hurt. The Christ Child is as anxious to eat as the Mother is anxious to feed Him. And so too the ample flowing breasts of God press down upon the gaping mouths of men.

Here is beatitude more than enough to quiet all the misery in the world!

All right, mankind, be miserable! Be lovely, be drunken, be sinful, and today draw down upon you this love without stint. Empty your stomachs in gluttony turned sick, empty your hearts in lust turned cold, empty your heads of hope unfounded, and God Incarnate will fill you.

Then proceed sick and sallow to the cave beneath the city. Find the Babe. Make Him comfortable. And then grow with Him in age and wisdom.

Editorial

In this issue we have attempted to bring home to our readers something of the mystery of Christmas. For all those who pray that some miracle will happen to change the course of history, some miracle that will stave off the disaster that threatens a world gone mad, be reassured, for this is it.

The happiness and harmony of men living in dignity, strong in their sufferings, great in their aspirations, that is not some idle dream, a vista beyond the years. The pattern and mark of God is already upon the affairs of men.

The miracles of God are always things of the present. God is now — not tomorrow. If the wills of men would quicken with a sudden and quiet "Yes," the thing would be done. The Kingdom of God, with its sufferings borne in joyous processional, would be here. A crack in the dykes of men's pride would let the sea of God's love come roaring in, for it is like that, a sea all about us, stretching to the horizon.

All of the complexities in the world of thought, theology shredded and garnished with apologetics, spiced with dogma, served with statistics and facts, dispersed by geniuses with the tongues of angels, cannot say more than what is said when we say, "Christ our Saviour is with us — today and forever."

THE EDITORS

Christmas is the merry time
    When greetings are in season,
And people send each other cards,
    With neither rhyme nor reason.

The Captive
A STORY

LIKE A PROPHET OF DISCONTENT, LIKE A scourging wind, rootless and bootless, Jonathan O'Hare roamed the darkening streets of Boston at eight o'clock on Christmas Eve. He glared at the hurrying people, he sniffed and jostled them; his mind picked them up like a twister, sucked them in, shredded them, dumped them helter-skelter into the great wriggling sack of memory. What he thought of them and their hurry he could have expressed in any one of seven languages. He chose English.

"Christ! What a fraud!" he was just off the boat from Greece. He hated these people because they were well-fed and well-clothed, well-soaped and well-oiled. Even their dead were well laid out; it was not much of a country for vultures. If it had not been for Charlie Raynor—

Charlie Raynor had sat on a swivel chair in Athens behind a desk polished within an inch of its life and spread his pudgy left hand flat on the desk so that the pale sunlight glinted on his big gold ring. On the ring it said: PRINCETON 1929. (What a year to be getting out of Princeton!) Charlie Raynor was a good bureau chief, but you couldn't talk to him.

"Butch," he had said, staring at his ring, "this isn't just a suggestion. It's an assignment. I'm assigning you to the States for six months."

"I like it here."

"I know you do. I know you don't want to go back; I don't understand it. You've been out of the country since before the war, since 1938. Don't you want to see your family?"

"I haven't got any. I'm an orphan."

Raynor's watery blue eyes swung up from the ring. "I didn't know. I'm sorry."

"Well, don't be. It won't do you or me any good."

"Don't you want to see your country again?"

"How do you know I have a country?"

"O'Hare, what's the matter? Have you got a girl you don't want to leave?"

"Sure; dozens I keep a house full of them," O'Hare retorted savagely.

Raynor stopped being chummy. "Listen, Butch, you're a good reporter; you're the best one I've got, and I don't want to lose you. I don't even want to lose you for six months. But you're working for an American newspaper, and you don't know what America's like any more. You've got to go back there for a while and — and — "

"Regain my perspective?" suggested O'Hare, quoting it.

"Yes, and get your bearings, and adjust your sights, and every other trite phrase you ever heard!"

O'Hare used his last weapon, the one that, he remembered, had always worked with his mother when she was still alive. He opened his eyes very wide, assumed the expression of a misunderstood school boy, and lamented: "Do I have to?"

"That or get out!" snapped Raynor, making a sharp knocking noise on the desk with his ring.

He hadn't wanted to get out; it was a good outfit to work for. It was a tie, and he had broken so many of them. So now he was padding along like an angry lion, sniffing and glaring and jostling and wanting to scratch eyes out. He walked faster, making his feet pound harder against the pavement, and every time they pounded it was the name of a country. India, China, Russia, France, Italy, Latvia, Finland — Christmas! Christ! What a fraud! In Kalgan the next morning some poor bastard was going to have his guts extracted by a bayonet while the missionaries were raising their Hosts on high; in Calcutta and Madras and Chabua children would be lying in the gutter starving, their bellies all puffed up, while the rich British and Anglo-Indians and the maharajas went roaring by in expensive American cars on their way to Christmas high tea; in Fiesole and Milan the young girls would be selling themselves on street corners for a warm bed to sleep in; all over Europe the DP's would grow one day older and staler. But here . . . here! Here people gave each other carefully wrapped presents and smirked:

"Merry Christmas!" The words came from an Irish girl and her husband brushing by O'Hare. They smiled broadly as they spoke, and he smiled back.

"Mala Kepi!" he shouted, grinning, saying a dirty thing in Mandarin. There they go, he thought, the blessed Irish (and I'm one of them!). Every third fat slob of an Irishman in the world tonight will tank up on beer, then crawl over to midnight Mass and tank up on sanctifying grace and go to bed glad that he's more thoroughly sanctified than the mockies and the wops and the commies. He will tumble out of bed in the morning, stub his toe, exclaim "Jesus Christ!" and then go tearing out of his house to shake people's hands and extend the season's greetings, with most of the sanctifying grace gone and some of the beer still sloshing around inside of him.

Not that there was anything wrong with going to midnight Mass, probably the best show any church in the world puts on. O'Hare had been an altar boy when he was young and still fell for that kind of stuff, and he could remember still the wonderful smell of incense, the way the candles smoked, the cramped little gurgles the kids on the altar let out before they fainted from excitement, the way the bishop looked when they took his shoes off, Father Riordan (or Devlin, or Halloran, or something like that; it didn't matter; he was one of those old Irish priests who would as soon spit on you as look at you) yelling "Hold it higher! Higher!" to the boy with the censer, and Father Sweeny going half crazy the time someone hid the tabernacle key. But the best of all was the music. O'Hare had cried once, kneeling on the sanctuary side of the altar rail in a row of kneeling boys, cried because the *Sanctus* was so beautiful. Even after he had stopped going to church he had thought sometimes that it might be a good idea to go in and just listen to the music. But he never had; all that crap about Christ had been hard to rub off, and he didn't want it to do over again.

O'Hare had slowed down to an ambling gait; he had even stopped reviling people. He was walking in a residential district where there were long rows of two-story brick houses like a child's blocks, each block with a square lawn in front of it, the combination looking like something out of a solid geometry class. A white Christmas would have made everything look much better, but there was no sign of snow; the night was clear and cold, like Angelina just before she walked out on him. The houses had wreaths hanging on their front doors and red electric candles burning in their downstairs windows and on the second floor the Christmas trees glowed and glittered.

Two kids were standing side by side at the pavement end of the front walk of one of the houses. As he passed them the boy darted quickly out in back of him and grasped his right hand; the girl did the same thing with his left. These kids were stronger than he was used to; instead of trying to shake them off he drew them forward so that he could see their faces.

"You're our captive!" they shrilled, self-consciously, laughing up at him but a little scared, now that pressure was being exerted on instead of by them. They were about thirteen. The boy was a red-head with a long face and narrow chin. He was wearing what was probably his first long-pants suit. The girl was brunette with dark brown eyes and a pug nose; she had a white party-dress on.

"What's this all about?" demanded O'Hare in a confidential tone.

"You have to come with us, Mister," said the boy. "We just captured you." He giggled.

"What for?"

"It's a game!" exclaimed the girl impatiently. "It's just like a scavenger hunt. Come on, now!" She tugged hopefully at his hand.

"Wait a minute, wait a minute," said O'Hare. "When I used to play in scavenger hunts all we had to bring back were things like cigarettes and soap dishes and backscratchers. Is this a new wrinkle?"

"Oh, we're the only ones who had to bring a *person* back," the boy answered. "It's because we're the oldest, and we let the younger kids make up the list. They said we had to capture the first person who passed by after we came outside the house and bring him back. You won't have to stay long," he declared. "We'll ransom you right away. Angelina and I—"

"What did you say?"

"Angelina—that's her name," the boy said, pointing at the girl.

"O.K. Let's go," said O'Hare.

"Hurrah!" cried Angelina.

"Wait a minute!" said O'Hare. "I might be—you know—a bad man. Are you sure you want me in your house?"

"That's the chance we're taking," the boy said seriously.

The three of them swung around so that Angelina was

on the outside and walked quickly toward the house. Now I'm scavenger bait! thought O'Hare. Was that how the other Angelina, the one who had been his wife, thought of him now? Well, he was giving the Angelinas of the world another chance: not that the first one had been precisely a bitch. She had been a pretty good egg, as a matter of fact; but living with her was like letting water drip on a stone until there's a big hole in the stone, it begins to split in the middle, and there's not much you can do with it except pick up the two pieces and throw them in different directions, as far as you can.

They reached the house. The front door was partly open. The boy gave it a push and O'Hare and Angelina walked through into a vestibule, then into a living room furnished in mahogany and dark red. There was a big charcoal sketch of a donkey minus tail on one wall, and a card table full of games in the center of the room beneath a sprig of mistletoe tied to the chandelier. In a fireplace with no vent an electric log burned forever. A scalloped tin disk, balanced delicately on a metal prong and revolved by hot air from the log, threw flickering shadows on the back of the fireplace.

"This is my house," said Angelina. "The others are my guests."

"What others?"

"Oh! They're all out scavenging — except George" — she nodded toward the red-head, who had stayed behind to shut the front door and now joined them — "and Mame. Mame!"

"What is it you're wanting now?" demanded a hostile voice from the rear of the house.

"Come and see our captive! What's your name, Mister? Jonathano Hayer? Oh! *Jonathan O'Hare!*"

A plump, middle-aged Irishwomen with a chin that could drive nails appeared, wiping her hands on her apron.

The Captive

"As if I didn't have enough to do," she sighed, "with your parents out and all your friends in, you have to start bringing perfect strangers into the house!" She put her hands on her wide hips. "And what is your mother going to say about *that*, I'd like to know?" She ignored O'Hare as if he were made of wood.

"Oh, Mame!" Angelina wailed dramatically. "We have only one captive and he's a very nice one, you can tell that by looking at him, and it's Christmas Eve, Mame! Shouldn't you invite strangers in on Christmas Eve?" She plays her cards well, thought O'Hare, like the other Angelina.

"Whoosh! Mister, you don't even look American. Are you a foreigner?"

"I was born here," answered O'Hare. "Right in this city. But I have been abroad. I arrived from Greece this afternoon."

"Oh!" exclaimed Angelina, delighted. "I bet you're rich and famous!"

"Neither. I'm a reporter."

"Ooooo! A foreign correspondent! Oh, George, what a wonderful captive! Oh, Mame!"

"Whoosh!" said Mame. "I have work to do. If you'll excuse me, me lady and gentlemen —." She nodded coolly to O'Hare, as if to say she didn't believe a word of his story, and retreated to the kitchen.

"Merry Christmas, Mame!" Angelina shouted after her. She grabbed O'Hare's hand. "Come on in and see where we're going to eat!" He followed her past the front door into the dining room. A long table was set with eight places. There was a single candle in a bronze candlestick at the near end.

"That's for the Gospel," said Angelina.

"My brother is in the seminary," George broke in, "and they won't let us go to midnight Mass. We're too young."

"And what has all that to do with the candle?" asked O'Hare.

"Well, don't you see? My brother in the seminary said it would be a good idea if we read the Gospel after we eat, since we can't go to midnight Mass."

People still fall for it, O'Hare thought a little tiredly, they still go for the antics at the altar and the trick clothes and the foreign language. They bring their children up to go for them too, they give their sons to the priesthood. He seized George by the collar.

"*You're* not going to run off to the seminary, are you?"

George looked up, surprised. "No, Mister. I want to be" — he smiled shyly — "a soldier, and go over the world."

O'Hare released his grip. "Learn Russian. It's the only language you'll need."

"Come in and sit down!" cries Angelina, pulling O'Hare back toward the living room. "The others will be here in a minute."

It was nearer ten minutes. Six of them, three boys and three girls, came hurtling through the front door together. They were all about twelve. They carried objects which they set down noisily on the card table — a goldfish bowl, two pieces of rye toast, a carrot dicer, a shoe horn, a bicycle bell.

"Look at our captive!" shouted Angelina, sitting next to O'Hare on a red leather couch. "He's a foreign correspondent and he just got back from Greece!" the children gathered around O'Hare, staring at his shoes, his clothes, his face. They looked at him as they might have looked at a wounded bird, or a silver dollar, or a mended fishnet.

"He's a *good* captive!"

"Hey, Mister, do they have Christmas in Greece?"

"So far as I know," said O'Hare, "they have Christmas everywhere."

"Do the children have parties and get presents? Do they believe in Santa Claus?"

"Some of them do. But most of them don't. And most of them don't believe in Santa Claus any more than you or I do. They start disbelieving a lot younger than we."

"Why?"

"Would you believe in Santa Claus very long if he never brought you anything?"

"I might," said Angelina. "I might believe that I had not been good enough for presents. I might believe that Santa Claus only had enough presents for the *very* good people."

"But you wouldn't feel very good about not getting anything."

"Of course I wouldn't. But what does that have to do with *believing*?"

"Would you charming children by any chance like to shovel some refreshments down your little throats?" demanded Mame, deceptively benevolent, standing in the dining room.

"Merry Christmas, Mame!" they chorused, and rushed for the dining room. Come *on*, Mr. O'Hare," said Angelina.

"I don't think Mame invited me."

Mame sniffed. "I set an extra place for you, Mr. O'Hare. I hope you don't object to American ice cream and cake."

O'Hare bowed gravely to Mame. "Mame," he said with a brogue, "you don't know how much pleasure it gives me to sit down to a table in me home country agin."

"Whoosh!"

"You sit here," insisted Angelina, leading him to the chair at the foot of the table and seating herself around the corner from him. George sat at the other end, the end with the candle. The lights in the living room had been turned off;

INTEGRITY: December, 1946

O'Hare and the children sat in the bright glow of an overhead light. Insulation, thought O'Hare, looking at it from the outer darkness where, he seemed to remember, a lot of weeping and gnashing of teeth went on. Or was that in the inner darkness? And what was the difference? The story had been something about a banquet, wedding feast, and some joker had shown up without his tux on and refused to go home and change. It was a good story.

"Cake," said Angelina, passing him a big platter. "What kind of cake do they have in Greece?"

"It isn't so good as this."

"Do they have ice cream?"

"In Athens," he said, thinking of the bread riots. "At the expensive hotels."

The children made an astonishing din eating. They clicked the ice cream spoons against their teeth, they banged mugs of hot chocolate on the table, they made scraping noises with forks on their cake plates, and they chattered constantly across the table, talking about new roller skates, new dresses, trains, all the things that they hoped would be theirs the next morning.

"*I* asked for a number two Erector set, and a handball glove, and—"

"You know, the kind with your initials on top?"

"Flexible Fliers are the best ones you can get."

At last they were finished, and Mame, commenting sarcastically, cleared the dishes away. "Is there anything else *you'd* like now, Mr. O'Hare?" she inquired truculently. O'Hare said nothing.

"It's time for the Gospel," said Angelina.

"Who's going to read it?" asked a girl in pink.

"George is. He's the oldest boy here."

"And besides," George put in, "it was my brother who gave us the idea." He got up and took a small New Testament from the sideboard. He sat down again, lit a match and applied it to the candle until the candle caught. Then he opened the book and found the place. He looked up expectantly.

"Wait," said Angelina. She rose, walked to a wall switch, and turned the overhead light off. The room dissolved into darkness except for a small circle of light where the candle was. "O. K.," she said. "Go ahead."

"Now it came to pass in those days," read George, "that there went forth a decree from Caesar Augustus that" — he stopped to clear his throat — "that a census of the whole world should be taken. This first census took place...." As he read, the candle flame jumped away from him, then back, throwing crazy shadows on the wall. His red hair glowed like dull embers. "... because there was no room for them in the inn. And there were shepherds..." He read it matter-of-factly, as if it were as real and obvious as a timetable, as a recipe, as a World Almanac. "And the angel said to them, 'Do not be afraid, for behold, I bring you good news...'" The shadow of the book was thrown on his face, so that the lower part of it was obscured and his nose and eyes and forehead reflected the bright yellow of the flame. "... and saying, 'Glory to God in the highest, and peace on earth among men of good will.'"

In the darkness it had been hard to tell who was weeping, but when Angelina turned the light on it was the captive, his face pillowed on his arms on the table, crying quietly and brokenly, like a child, like a person who hadn't cried in a long time, like a lost soul.

JOHN R. MCCARTHY
New York City
October 1946

INTEGRITY: December, 1946

At Christmas office-party time
    The bosses are less haughty,
In democratic songs they chime,
    And sometimes get quite naughty.

Integrity
Incarnate

"I will place enmities between thee and the woman, and thy seed and her seed."
Genesis iii, 15.

IN THE CHRISTIAN VIEW OF HISTORY, there are four figures outstanding; two who appear at the inception of the human story and two who appear in the fullness of time—Adam and Eve, Christ and Mary. To those outside the Church this may seem an extraordinary simplification of the vast and complex panorama of human lives and human destinies. It is, of course, a simplification, because the Christian view is taken from the vantage point of the divine Mind revealed in Sacred Scripture. It is also the most profound view, because human history, not so much as recorded but as lived, is the working out of the divine Plan for the external manifestation of God's glory. It is, moreover, an optimistic view that does not overlook the evil in the story; its optimism is motivated by the omnipotence of God, Who, it believes, can and does always bring good out of the evil He permits. When writing the story, the human mind confronts countless cases in which it can not see the good springing from the evil permitted; nevertheless, in the pivotal events of the story—in the Fall of man and his Redemption, the power of God's mercy to bring good out of evil is inescapable.

THE HUMAN STORY BEGINS WITH AN INTEGRAL man, dissatisfied with his God-given integrity, who wanted to be like God, to be the end of his own integral perfection. The story reaches its climax with a Divine Person, who thought it no robbery to assume the nature and form of a man that he might restore the integrity of human nature by lifting it to an intimate commerce with the divine nature. The perfection of human nature was lost by a personal act of its first possessor, Adam; a greater perfection was bestowed upon it by a personal union with the Son of God. Shattered human integrity gave place to Incarnate Integrity.

But this is trying to say too much in too few words; though no amount of words can unveil the mystery of the Fall and the Redemption. However, we should try to follow more slowly the sequence of events that contains these mysteries.

The Redemptive Incarnation is not a divine afterthought; Christ is not a trouble-shooter sent to straighten out an unexpected breakdown in the machinery of creation. Christ—the Incarnate Redeemer—is the first-born of angels and men. God had no need to create; but if He willed to create, it could be only to manifest exteriorly His inner glorious perfection. He had no choice of the motive for creating. Moreover, it was according to His Wisdom to choose the best way of attaining the end of creation. God saw that the best way to manifest His glory to man was the way of mercy. This was the way He chose. God could have willed, for example, that Adam and Eve and all their posterity should remain sinless and that Christ and Mary should appear near the end of time.

Yet, contrary to what we might suppose, such unspotted goodness would not manifest the divine perfection as gloriously as the goodness brought about by the grace of God despite the sins of men. So while we contemplate the first man and woman as they came from the hands of God, we must keep in mind that their perfection before they sinned, is but a dim reflection of what God intended to pour out on Christ and Mary.

APART FROM THE INCARNATION, THE MAKING OF man was the most delicate task of God's creative work. For man was to be the bridge between two universes—the visible universe of minerals, plants, and animals, and the invisible universe of the angelic hierarchy. Actually, there is but one universe, visible and invisible, with man as the link between the parts; for man is the highest of the animals and the lowest of the spirits. Each man is one being; yet he is a composite being and the parts that compose him are not completely transformed by their union. Matter does not become spirit, nor spirit matter; matter and spirit become one man. Man has a body that is a human body; that is, it sums up within itself the mineral, plant, and animal kingdoms, yet it is a fit instrument of the soul for human living. Man's soul is spiritual, yet not angelic, for its natural perfection, though not its existence, depends upon the body.

MAN'S—A LIMITED PERFECTION

In uniting matter and spirit to make man, God produced the most perfect creature of the visible universe, the king of material creation. Nevertheless, man's is a very limited perfection. There are several signs of this limitation of human nature and of the human persons that subsist in that nature.

Thus, while man's soul is immortal, man's body, composed of many elements that tend to disintegrate, is mortal. Man, the composite of spirit and matter, is then naturally mortal. While his being as man demands that body and soul remain forever united, there is no natural power within him that can stay the dissolution of his body or ward off the eventual approach of death.

Being within the material universe, man has to be equipped to take his place therein. The material universe is composed of objects that are visible, audible, tangible, smellable, tastable. These same objects are either good or bad for the rest of material creation. Man, therefore, was equipped with external and internal senses that give him an awareness of the whole universe around him and with sense appetites that respond to the good and evil in his environment. However, the same senses that can enjoy the beauty and goodness of the universe can also be horrified by its ugliness and evil. The same nerves that give man the capacity for sensual pleasure can bring to consciousness the sting of pain. If man is to have eyes that may delight in the beauty of a sunset, he must also run the risk of blindness, for the eyes are organs of a body that is subject to disease and death.

COMPLEX HUMAN NATURE IS SUBJECT TO another serious limitation, of which we are all constantly aware. This is the conflict between what we call our "higher" and "lower" natures, between the "spiritual man" and the "animal man." In us this conflict is due to the sin of Adam for a reason that we shall soon see. Yet it must be admitted that the root of the conflict lies in human nature itself. Man is a creature whose perfection must be outside himself, in the attainment of something other than himself. His search for perfection calls into service all the powers of his soul and body, for the perfection of his nature is also a complex thing. There is good and evil for his soul, good and evil for his body.

The good of the whole man and the special good of his soul are sought by his spiritual faculties, the intellect and the will. Particular goods that serve the needs of man's body and indirectly, of his soul are sought by the exterior and interior faculties of man: sight, taste, smell, imagination, memory, and so forth; and by the sense appetites, whose activities we call love, hate, fear, hope and so forth.

Now all these faculties of man should cooperate amicably to obtain the fullness of human perfection. Yet they can fall out and go off on their own. Any number of instances will occur to us. Take, for example, the conflict that may arise in a Catholic who walks into a restaurant on Friday evening. He knows that for his own good the Church has focused his obligation to mortify himself in the precept of Friday abstinence, among other precepts. His mind has long ago assented to this command as something good for man. However, this submission of the spirit does not blind the eyes, lock up the ears, or stop up the nose when the waiter passes with a sizzling steak; rather there is a spontaneous rising of desire in the lower nature, the imagination adds the pleasures of taste and satisfied stomach, and the sense appetites respond without consulting the intellect and will. As there is, in fact, a conflict between the *spiritual, universal good* of mortification and the *particular, sensible good* of a steak dinner, there will be a similar conflict within a man who is presented with a choice of these two goods. There is a natural conflict that stems from the complex nature of human perfection. The higher good should always be preferred to a lower good that conflicts with it; nevertheless, this does not prevent the lower good from presenting its claims and enlisting the animal appetites in its own behalf. The final decision has to be made by the will, which too often gives in to the inordinate demands of the animal appetites and becomes guilty of sin. The will is never forced to give in, but it is normally forced to put up a battle for the claims of the spiritual good of man.

One more human limitation need be mentioned here. Ordinarily, man comes into existence without knowledge of himself or others; his mind is a complete blank, although it is capable of tremendous development. The acquisition of truth is always a long process for the human mind, though it was not intended by God to be a laborious one.

We have pointed out four great limitations that are of the very nature of man:
1) Mortality
2) The capacity to suffer
3) The tension and conflict between the spiritual and the animal in man
4) The necessity of slowly acquiring the knowledge needed to live well

None of these limitations was to be found in Adam and Eve as they were first made by God; they were free from the menace of death or suffering, spared conflict between sense and reason, appetite and will, possessed knowledge suitable to their position as chiefs of creation and progenitors of the human race.

HOW WAS THIS ACCOMPLISHED?

How was this integral perfection of human nature accomplished? By special gifts that are called preternatural because they do not belong properly to human nature, but to angelic nature. This does not mean that God turned men into angels; He did grant to man certain privileges that brought him closer to angelic perfection while always remaining human.

Of these four gifts, one, the gift of knowledge, was given to Adam and Eve personally; it was not to be inherited by their children who would start life without any knowledge just as children do today. Special knowledge was granted to the first man and woman because they were first, because they started their human career as adults.

The three other gifts established human nature as integral; one of them, however, which submitted the lower nature to the dictates of reason and grace, is called specifically the gift of integrity. All three were not personal gifts but were given to Adam and Eve as possessors and propagators of human nature. They were, therefore, to be inherited by all who were born of Adam and Eve. Human generation is a process whereby two human persons, male and female, cooperate with God in the production of a third human person by handing on a human nature to their offspring. The parents transmit the human nature as they possess it; if, in them, it were still adorned with preternatural gifts, they would hand down an integral human nature; if they have lost the integrity of their own nature by sin, they hand down a nature that is likewise unintegrated.

THE GREATEST GIFT—GRACE

The preternatural gifts were given to human nature in Adam and Eve not simply to overcome the limitations of that nature, but to dispose it and human persons possessing it, most perfectly for God's greatest gift to man — the supernatural life of grace. Integral human nature without grace would be at the summit of natural perfection; it would not have a share in God's own perfection. However, God wished that man attain even to this high perfection; He wanted man to be eternally happy by possessing the same object that made

Him happy — the infinite Goodness of God Himself. Such perfection is not natural to any creature, man or angel; it is natural only to God, supernatural to all others. It can, however, be won by creatures through the power of grace working on and with free will.

It was God's intention that all children of man should be born in grace; He would give grace to every child born with an integral nature. Just as now He always creates and infuses a spiritual soul into the matter disposed by the parents, so, in His original plan, He would have at the same instant infused grace into the soul that was to be a part of an integral human nature. This was to be the glorious heritage of the sons of man — to be sons of God from their birth as men. Each would then have to pass the same test established for Adam and Eve, the test of humility and obedience. Each would receive an eternal reward in heaven when the test had been successfully passed. As long as each man remained subject to God, he would retain the preternatural integrity of his nature and rejoice in the special friendship of God. But if he rebelled against God, grace would depart from his soul and the preternatural gifts would be stripped from his nature. By contrition and penance he could regain the grace of God, but his nature would never again possess its original integrity. He could hand down to his children only the inheritance of sin, for now they would come into the world with a nature stripped of its integrity and therefore deprived of the sanctifying grace that would make them pleasing to God, bearing within them the penalty of their father's rebellion.

Adam's sin was a personal sin; yet it had its effect on the whole of human nature, because it shattered the integrity of that nature in him who was to be its source in all others.

WHY?

At this point of the human story the mind is always tempted to ask—Why? Why did God allow His masterpiece to be defaced? Why did He even create man when He knew beforehand that man's sin would destroy His work in so short a time? We know the answer, though we have only the dark evidence of faith for its cogency. God had in mind the production of an even greater masterpiece, whose magnificence could be best brought out by contrast with the despoiled original. Moreover, God had in the beginning poured out His gifts on man, asking in return only that man recognize the fact that his perfection came from God and could come from God alone. Man was not convinced. Eve did not spurn the suggestion that the divine prohibition was thrown around the Tree of Knowledge because God was afraid of man. How, then, could man be convinced of God's goodness, except by being deprived of its fruits? If man would not be grateful for a perfection that came to him almost automatically at birth, perhaps he would respond to a perfection that was achieved through the bloody death of a God-Man on the Cross and his own unceasing efforts under the inspiration of the grace that flowed from the Cross.

> When God arose upon the red mountains
> > Man had fallen prone
> Flat and flung wide like a continent, capes and headlands,
> > The vast limbs thrown.
> And the Lord lamented over Man, saying "Never
> > Shall there be but one
> For no man born shall be mighty as he was mighty
> > To amaze the sun.

INTEGRITY: December, 1946

> Not till I put upon me the red armour
>   That was man's clay
> And walk the world with the mask of man for a vizor
>   Not till that day.
> For on God alone shall the image of God be graven
>   Which Adam wore
> Seeing I alone can lift up this load of ruin
>   To walk once more."[1]

The human nature that lost its integrity and supernatural rectitude by the sin of Adam was infinitely exalted by its union with the Person of the Son of God. Even in Christ, by a free act of His Divine Will, the gifts of immortality and impassibility were not restored, because He wished to become like us in all things save sin. But there was perfect integrity in the complexity of Christ's human nature, wrought by its substantial union with a Divine Person and by the treasures of grace bestowed upon it by God. As Adam came into the world pure and holy, so did Christ. One other also came in like manner. As the first-fruit of the Redemption, Mary, the new Eve, Christ's Mother and Helpmate, was freed from any taint of the original sin and its effects.

All others were to attain the life of grace not by birth, but by rebirth, not from their human parents handing down the heritage of Adam and Eve, but from their spiritual parents, the New Adam and the New Eve, Christ and Mary. From the moment Adam and Eve regained the grace of God until the last man or woman passes out of life, human integrity is not to be a gift given at birth, but a prize awarded for a continual struggle within each man between grace and his spiritual

---

[1] G.K. Chesterton, *The Return of Eve*

nature on the one hand and sin and his animal nature on the other. Perfect integrity, that is, complete subordination of the lower nature to the demands of reason and grace is always beyond man in this life; it was a special privilege of Christ and Mary. A degree of integrity can be won through prayer, penance and the grace of Christ.

OF GOD'S MERCY

This is God's final attempt to convince man that he is a creature of God's mercy. In mercy He created man, in mercy He forgave him his original rebellion, in mercy He redeemed him, in mercy He regenerates him, in mercy He strengthens him during the battle of life, in mercy and in mercy alone He will save him at the last. If, in his pride, man rejects God's mercy, he rejects God. If man rejects God finally, he loses the last hope of regaining his integrity and heads through the gates of eternal conflict.

JAMES M. EGAN, O.P.
Sparkill, N.Y.
October, 1946

CELEBRATION

Christmas is gone again, O Christ,
Thy birth's commemoration is a tree
Drunkenly askew upon a too-full garbage can.

Dear God! how we held Thy day! There never was
Such feasting. Turkey-stuffed, wineful men
Swapped stories till the wild guffaws rumbled
The very roof. What tales! And the pretty girls!
Red-lipped and their dark hair curled they came
Because it was Your Birthday and they knew
There would be boys, and mistletoe and a going home
In the dark. How we hurled Thy name
Loud-voiced across the noisy crowd
Who ate and danced and sang and laughed
With us to think that You were born!
O Lord! You never saw such merriment.

Christmas is gone again. Again
Thy birth's commemoration is a tree.
O Lord God, Merciful God! were pressed thorns harder
And a bloody death than this? Can it be
Easier to hang tinsel-bound to a toy tree
And a heartbroken die again of mockery? O God,
Father of Christ, spare us who flout Thy Son.

JIM SHAW

INTEGRITY: December, 1946

IN BETHLEHEM[1]

O Christmas is a merry time,
    The bells go ting-a-ling.
O Christmas is a merry time,
    The little birdies sing.
O Christmas is a merry time,
    The street-cars go ding-ding.
O Christmas is a merry time,
    I'll bet you anything.

O Christmas is a merry time,
You thought I couldn't find a rhyme!
Change two nickels for a dime.
Listen to the cow-bells chime!
How high can a monkey climb?
Does every man return to slime?
And isn't it an awful crime
That Christmas is a merry time?

O Christmas is a merry time,
The very time
Poor Tom's a-cold.
    Each sound that falls
    O'er Bedlam's walls
    Divinely calls
    Through padded stalls
    'Poor Tom's a-cold!'
In Bedlam's halls
Poor Tom's a-cold
In Summer time.
And Christmas is a merry time.
    Poor Tom's a-cold.

O Christmas is a merry time,
A fairy time.
To think of it!
    A single star,
    Tho' e'er so far,
    Can hold ajar
    The prison bar.
    To think of it!
What fools men are
To think of it
At any time.
And Christmas is a merry time
    To think of it.

O Christmas is a merry time,
A merry time
In Bedlam town.
    All grief is shorn,
    All sorrow torn
    From every horn
    And left forlorn
    In Bedlam Town.
For Christ was born
In Bedlam Town
At Christmas time.
And Christmas is a merry time
    In Bedlam Town.

IN BETHLEHEM

O Christmas is a merry time,
Bet two nickels to a dime,
Bet I know a man can climb
High enough to find a rhyme
For chime and thyme and
    Christmas time.
That's a lot above the slime,
And I maintain it is no crime
That Christmas is a merry time.

O Christmas is a merry time,
    And Time's a merry trick,
O Christmas is a merry time,
    The bells go tick-tock-tick,
O Christmas is a merry time,
    Eternities are quick,
O Christmas is a merry time,
    To be a lunatic.

JIM SHAW

[1] *The setting for the poem is Bedlam, the hospital of St. Mary of Bethlehem in London, long used as a hospital for lunatics.*

UNITED NATIONS ASSEMBLY

UPSTAIRS AND DOWN

Case 13,013

From Rev. Nahum Priest to Mrs. Rebecca Doeg, Executive Secretary of the Jericho Family Welfare Society

Tishri 12

Dear Mrs. Doeg:

Yesterday I had a most distressing experience. Returning from Jerusalem to Jericho, I saw a man lying unconscious by the roadside whom I recognized as a certain Jeroboam who is employed at Simeon's tannery. He had evidently fallen among robbers who also stripped him and having wounded him and went away leaving him half dead.

Since I have never had a course in First Aid, there was obviously nothing I could do about the case at the moment. Therefore I am referring the matter to the Family Welfare Society. Will you kindly send one of your case workers to visit Mr. Jeroboam and to aid in his rehabilitation?

Sincerely,

NAHUM PRIEST

From Mrs. Rebecca Doeg to Rev. Nahum Priest

Tishri 19

Reverend and dear Sir:

I have your letter of Tishri 12 referring to our agency the case of a Mr. Jeroboam who was robbed on the Jerusalem-Jericho Turnpike. By a coincidence the same case was also referred by Mr. Samuel Levite whom you doubtless know. I assure you the case will receive our prompt attention.

May I take this occasion to discuss another matter with you? As you are aware, the plans for the annual campaign of the Jericho Community Fund are now being drawn up. We are anxious to have the allotment of the Family Welfare Society increased from 45,000 denarii, the present figure, to 50,000 denarii. Mr. Abdias, a close friend of yours, is a member of the Budget Committee of the Fund. Would you use your good offices with him in favor of the increased allotment?

It is urgently necessary to increase the present salary scale of our agency. Unless we pay higher salaries we cannot continue to attract the type of highly trained professional social workers which our standards require.

Sincerely,

REBECCA DOEG.

From Rev. Nahum Priest to Mrs. Rebecca Doeg

Cheshvan 1

Dear Mrs. Doeg:

I have been seeking an opportunity to bring up the matter you mention with Mr. Abdias — but thus far unsuccessfully. It is scarcely necessary for me to tell you that I am enthusiastically in favor of the increased allotment. You have done a fine job with the Family Welfare Society and I feel that the citizens of Jericho owe you their fullest support.

By the way, have you any report on the Jeroboam case which I referred to you on Tishri 12?

Sincerely,

NAHUM PRIEST.

From Mrs. Rebecca Doeg to Rev. Nahum Priest

Cheshvan 8

Reverend and dear Sir:

The Jeroboam case is being handled by Miss Sophonias who is at present away on vacation. As soon as she returns I shall forward to you a full report.

Many thanks for your friendly support. I hope you will soon be able to contact Mr. Abdias.

Sincerely,

REBECCA DOEG.

From Rev. Nahum Priest to Mrs. Rebecca Doeg

Kislev 12

Dear Mrs. Doeg:

I finally ran into Mr. Abdias yesterday and discussed the matter of the increased allotment for the Family Welfare Society. I found him most sympathetic. He said that several people had already brought the matter to his attention and he expects favorable action when the Budget Committee meets next week.

Please do not think me importunate, but have you any report yet on the Jeroboam case?

Sincerely.

NAHUM PRIEST.

From Miss Judith Aggeus to Rev. Nahum Priest

Kislev 15

Reverend and dear Sir:

Your letter to Mrs. Doeg, dated Kislev 12, arrived while she was out of the city. I shall bring it to her attention immediately on her return. I am sure she will deeply appreciate your kindness in securing the favorable interest of Mr. Abdias.

The Jeroboam case has been referred to the Travelers Aid Society.

Respectfully,

JUDITH AGGEUS
Secretary to Mrs. Doeg.

INTEGRITY: December, 1946

From Mrs. Rebecca Doeg to Rev. Nahum Priest

Kislev 22

Reverend and dear Sir:

I have just returned from Jerusalem where I attended a very successful meeting of the Palestinian Conference of Social Work. Miss Sophonias of our agency read a paper on "Psychosomatic Factors in the Adjustment of Patients Suffering from Multiple Contusions" which was very well received.

How very good of you to use your influence with Mr. Abdias! I have been given to understand that the Budget Committee acted favorably on our request. I wish I could tell you how very grateful we are to socially minded persons like yourself.

The Travelers Aid Society do not feel that they should handle the Jeroboam case which was referred to them by our agency. I am planning to take up the matter with Miss Phanuel, Executive Secretary of the Travelers Aid Society.

Sincerely,

REBECCA DOEG.

From Rev. Nahum Priest to Mrs. Rebecca Doeg

Tebet 21

Dear Mrs. Doeg:

It is now more than three months since I referred the Jeroboam case to you and I have yet to hear that you have done anything on it. Can't you give me some sort of a report?

Sincerely,

NAHUM PRIEST.

Case 13,013

From Mrs. Rebecca Doeg to Rev. Nahum Priest

Shebat 12

Reverend and dear Sir:

In reply to yours of Tebet 21 I submit the following report on the Jeroboam case.

At a conference with Miss Phanuel of the Travelers Aid Society the Jeroboam case was thoroughly discussed. I was not successful in persuading Miss Phanuel that the case should be handled by her agency, but at least the conference resulted in considerable clarification of thought.

Later I brought the matter up for discussion at a staff meeting of my workers. The upshot of the meeting was that we should not proceed further without consulting our Board.

At the next Board meeting I presented the case of Mr. Jeroboam in some detail. The Board members agreed that the Travelers Aid Society had been rather uncooperative. It was unanimously voted that we should stand firm in our position since, if we should now reopen the case after referral to Miss Pahnuel, it would establish a dangerous precedent.

Please excuse my delay in sending you this report. All of us at the office have been desperately busy with preparations for the coming Community Fund campaign.

Sincerely,

REBECCA DOEG.

From Rev. Nahum Priest to Mrs. Rebecca Doeg

Adar 25

Dear Mrs. Doeg:

I acknowledge your letter of Shebat 12. Being, I confess, somewhat troubled in my conscience, I took it upon myself to visit Mr. Jeroboam personally, a step which I now regret.

INTEGRITY: December, 1946

According to Jeroboam's story, it seems that some time after the robbery a certain Samaritan being on his journey came near to him, and seeing him was moved with compassion, and going up to him bound up his wounds pouring in oil and wine, and setting him upon his own beast brought him to an inn and took care of him, and the next day he took out two denarii and gave to the host and said, "Take care of him and whatsoever thou shalt spend over and above, I, at my return will repay thee."

As we discussed the matter further Jeroboam became more and more unreasonable. When he learned that I had seen him by the roadside he demanded why I, a priest, could not have done as much for him as the Samaritan did. I managed to keep my temper and explained to him as patiently as I could that personally I had no special competence to handle cases like his and that I had referred the matter to the Family Welfare Society so that highly trained professional social workers could render him the expert assistance which he needed.

When I mentioned the Family Welfare Society, Jeroboam launched into a diatribe on social work in general and the Family Welfare Society in particular. He claimed that in the five months since the robbery no social worker had even visited him and held this up as an example of the inefficiency of social agencies. He added that he was perfectly well able to manage his own affairs "without any social workers butting into my business," as he uncouthly expressed it.

Before I could manage to get away, he treated me to quite a lecture on his half-baked social philosophy. He felt that everyone has an obligation to love everyone else. We should all help one another even to the extent of impoverishing ourselves — and so on *ad nauseum*. He even had the audacity to hold the Samaritan up as an example to me, a priest! Between ourselves, I suspect the fellow of radical leanings. Perhaps he has even been listening to this Jesus of Nazareth whose influence is causing so much dangerous unrest.

I hope you will be kind enough to overlook my rather hasty letter of Tebet 21. The enclosed check for 25 denarii is my contribution to the Community Fund. I trust it will not be too late.

Sincerely,

NAHUM PRIEST.
PAUL HANLY FURFEY
Catholic University,
Washington, D. C.
October 1946

The Gift Is Ours

WHATEVER ITS ENEMIES MAY SAY ABOUT the Faith, they cannot say it is dull. It is not static. It is not lifeless. It is dramatic in its saints and dramatic in its symbols. The Cathedral at Chartres is dramatic. St. Francis of Assisi is dramatic. Even the least of the Faith make contact with the Church at the most moving and poignant times of their lives: when they are born, when they marry, and when they are dying. When men move most gloriously or most fiercely, they move for or against the Faith. The strongest men choose her as their Lady or as the Beast they would slay. It is not strange that the march of men bravely should be called a crusade, or that before them they should carry the Cross. Saint Francis went down the Nile; Saint Isaac Jogues went down the St. Lawrence. Both moved into the camp of the enemy, and before them went the Cross.

The sign of the Cross is the sign of men acting as God, humbly without fear. The Cross is the most dynamic symbol in the history of man. Whenever or wherever the Wood has been crossed with steel, the steel has been lowered, and the Wood triumphant. Men chained to the days of their petty years fail to see this, but history tells the story. As the Cross was raised all other symbols bowed before it. The Roman fasces is romance revived yesterday only to die again. The Crescent of Islam is pale in the East. The barbed arrow of the Hun is waked in the museums of Christendom. That mark of sorcery, the swastika, has been returned to the harmless pattern of the ouija board.

Now, today there are two vile symbols dark against the sky. It is evening for one; midday for the other: in the West the Dollar Sign; in the East the Hammer and Sickle. These will be history as the Cross moves on.

THE GROWTH OF THE CROSS

Do not be fooled by the cross sculptured upon a wall or chained to the necks of women. That is the cross of the artist or the sculptor, fossilized, imprisoned in wood, stone or metal. The Cross of Christ lives and grows. It has life and motion. Let me show you. Here are the diagrams:

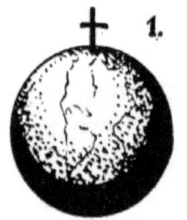

1) The Cross surmounts the world. See from what activity the symbol of the Cross emerges! Let it grow as it must: eastward, westward, earthward, and heavenward.

2) Stretching out its arms horizontally, the Cross grows and encircles the world. Plunging downward, passing through the center of the earth, it comes out on the other side. It is now the axis upon which the planet rotates. There is a soaring upward as the upper arm rockets even to the throne of God. Now we have a circle and an axis. The circle is this: the movement of man historically from Adam until now. It is man as man, earthbound, traveling parallel with the earth's surface, ever subjected to the mood of nature, of seed, of sun, of rain and stars. That is the stretched-out, ever growing horizontal bar of the Cross. The axis is this: It is Divinity. It is God creating, sustaining, nurturing, moving and loving His Creation. It is God reflected in matter, in rocks, minerals, waters, plants, animals, and upward into the realm of man, beyond man to the angels.

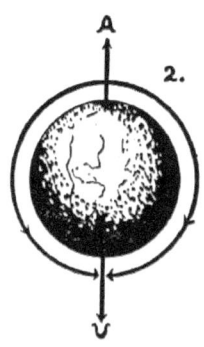

And what is the point of intersection, that spot where the horizontal crosses the vertical forming our Cross? That is the Incarnation! That is the magnificent story that begins with "Ave Maria" and ends with "He is risen!" It is the sublime mystery of God told in words understandable to children. It is God coming forth from the womb of a virgin. All the temporality of man and all the energy of the universe meet and combine with the Being of God. And His name is Emmanuel, God with us!

There is a mystery greater still in its meaning for us for which a diagram is a presumption. The mystery is this, as Christ has revealed it to us: there is nothing of time and God, for He is always. We do not speak the whole truth if we say God was born, as though the Incarnation was merely an historical event.

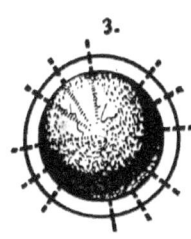

The effects of the Incarnation, of man being joined with God, are eternally *present* in the activities of mankind. Christmas is not an historical celebration. It is the Incarnation *made present*. Thus, in the diagram (3), with dotted lines I have indicated that everywhere, ever-present is the confluence and wedding of God with Man, in Christ.

I LOVE A MYSTERY

Somewhere in the East, I am told, the faithful have hung before their altars a shimmering curtain of silver. According to their strange liturgy it is customary to gaze upon this curtain until an hypnotic state is produced. This trance is their form of worship. We of Western Christendom have not been untouched by the poisonous mysticism of the Orient. In a second-hand book store in Boston I found, on a shelf marked "The Occult," a treatise of Aquinas. A man who had the most active of intellects, one who was in the most real sense *conscious,* is classified among those who seek their beatitude in oblivion!

The Christian mysteries are not productive in inertia. The Faith is a love affair between God and man. No lover is repelled by the mystery of his beloved. John Jones does not say of bewitching Mary Smith, "She's a mystery and that's the end of it," and then go out and court some shallow-minded imbecile. A man who is thirsty is not saddened by the dimensions of a mountain lake. He does not say, "That's more water than I can drink," and then lie down upon the bank unquenched. We can and should always drink our fill of the mysteries of God. It is because He is God that there is more mystery than we can encompass. So it is with the mystery of Christ's Incarnation. To know one thing about Christ is to know a million things about His universe.

Now that I have embarked upon this great sea of mystery, do not think for a moment that I can explain its immensity. When I say that but one thing is needed — everything, do not anticipate my saying everything that can be said about it. All that I am trying to say is that this mystery of the Incarnation explains the first principle which moves the universe of angels and devils, of cabbages and kings. Breaking the universe down into test tubes will not reveal the first Thing about it: why it goes, and goes the way it does. The reason and cause of the universe and everything in it resides in the Mind of God. It is in the mysteries of Faith that these first causes are revealed to us. Without a knowledge of these mysteries we know nothing about anything (as far as it pertains to our supernatural life). These mysteries are the lever with which we can move the earth. If I could apply the knowledge gained by Faith to four totally different aspects of living, by implication we might catch a tiny glimpse of that totality which is Christ.

ON BREAD

Where man is you will find bread. It is in the *Our Father*. It is in the grocery store. It is on the altars of our churched. The making of bread is the world's largest industry. Last year men made millions on wheat. Man does not live by bread alone — he can't live without it.

In Bethlehem (which means house-or-bread) a seed of wheat was sown. It was put in the earth and it died. From this death the life of the wheat emerged. Of this wheat many loaves of bread were made. With seven of the loaves Christ fed four thousand people. The Son of God Himself ate one of these loaves, and that wheat became Christ. The seed died and became wheat; the wheat died and became Christ. Within the wheat there was something of the earth, there was something of the air and the rain. As Christ consumed this wheat He consumed the things of which it was constituted, and these things returned to God through Christ. That is how Christ redeems matter: by making it one with Himself.

On Holy Thursday, taking bread He gave thanks, and broke, and gave to them, saying, *This is My body which is given for you.* The disciples took it. They ate of Christ. Men ate of Divinity.

Can we comprehend the marvel of all this — the wonder of all these things of time and space being made one in Christ? Here are the Things of God taking place within the homely realm of the dinner table. Just think of the blasphemy, that after these mysteries have been revealed, men can go about the business of growing, buying and selling wheat, unconcerned with the Incarnation! Does this not cast some light upon today's iniquity in regard to the economy of wheat? Can these social problems be explained or corrected apart from the mysteries of Faith? —

1) That rich wheat lands are the causes of wars?
2) That our popularly consumed white bread is without the nourishment of wheat, and is the cause of degenerative disease?
3) That men walk into the lavatories of the grain-market and blow out their brains?
4) That the greedy production of wheat for market is making of our Midwest an arid desert?

Ignoring Christ, men have forgotten the first principle of life in the universe. The blessing of wheat, perverted by avarice, unthanked before God, has become a curse. Instead of nourishing, it starves. Instead of uniting men, it brings wars between them. Instead of life, it brings death.

ON AN ANNUAL WAGE

The desire of working men for an annual wage is a desire for security. I have not the space to discuss this matter on the politico-economic level, nor is that my intention. I only hope to relate this idea to a unified concept of an economy generated by Christ. It is just as important for a unionist to know what security is as it is for a philosopher to know its definition. If the worker does not know what he wants, how can he expect to get it? It is still a complex question as to whether an annual wage will give the worker what he really needs.

The temporal security of man proceeds from his "looking to the Kingdom of Heaven and its justice." If he does this,

Christ assures him that "all these things will be added unto you." To say that this doctrine has no economic significance is blasphemy. It would be making a mockery of the Lord's Prayer in which we ask God for our daily bread.

When a man looks to the Kingdom of Heaven and its justice he does all of these things:

1) He believes that he is sustained and nurtured in all his temporal needs by an Almighty and All-Merciful Father.
2) He works with his hands the things that are good and to the benefit of his neighbors.
3) He elects and furthers an economy of distributive justice wherein he places the common good before his own good or the good of his family.
4) He considers the well-being of all those who are less than he (whether in talent, physical health, intelligence, moral courage, or wealth) as his responsibility, and he does for them what he is able.
5) He seeks to grow in understanding of God's justice by prayer and meditation and frequent reception of the Sacraments.
6) He is in our time a lay apostle.

Failing to seek these ends, a man may still achieve an abundance of worldly goods, but he does so at the expense of the common good. The common good cannot be attained apart from the Will of God for His children. The good of any one man is not to be sought apart from the common good. Acting within these boundaries outlined here, any man can be assured that his security lies in God's hands and that he is at the same time advancing the prosperity of society. Thus equipped, he can take the matter of an annual wage in hand, judge it for what it is worth, and act accordingly.

THE JEW

In the economy of Christ, the Jew is our neighbor and we will be judged in accordance with our justice in his regard. It is our obligation to see that the Jew is respected as one of the chosen race whence Christ issued. The mystery of the survival of the Jew in spite of every obstacle in his path, more often than not placed in his way by uncharitable Christians, is a religious mystery. Do not forget that it is the vocation of that nation to be restored to Christ.

Anti-Semitism among Catholics today is a disgrace to the Church. In no way is it related to their being Catholics. Catholicism can have no part with hatred or injustice, and it is certainly an injustice to brand a group with the sins of some of its members. As long as Christians nurture the belief that their well-being is part and parcel of a jungle economy, then will they be tempted to hatred and envy of those more successful than they in its savage pursuits. It is in the field of trade and finance that Anti-Semitism flourishes. It is much less among those men who labor with their hands, or in intellectual or cultural circles. Nothing could do more to eliminate intolerance or envy than the knowledge that one's material prosperity as well as that of society as a whole can best be achieved though Christian charity. This is the unifying force of the Incarnation.

ON THE HOUSING PROBLEM

Lack of housing facilities in the United States would not have become so acute had there been due concern for charity and justice on the part of politicians. The truth of the matter is that there has been a serious housing problem for the last fifty years, but the shortage until recently has been the lot of inarticulate minorities. Lacking organization, these people have had no lobbies in Washington nor in their state capitols. Having little money, their plight was ignored by the merchants (for they were not prospective customers). Consequently, the voice of the press was not raised in their behalf. The share cropper and the tenant farmer of the south and west lacked adequate houses. The slum dwellers of our large cities have been without decent facilities. Negroes and other racial minorities have been confined by poverty and prejudice to over-crowded city tenements. Had our press and public been more concerned about these unfortunates, the demand for more houses would have been raised long before this. Now that the epidemic has spread to the upper classes there is a frightful hue and cry. It is still a question of each seeking what is his own without concern for the common good.

The selfishness of labor unions and capitalists alike have contributed to this mess. This housing shortage existed while union halls were crowded with unemployed carpenters, and architects were selling apples on the streets of Manhattan. On the one hand the building-trade unions, placing wages before dignity, enforced ridiculous restrictions upon their workers. The inviolability of craft boundaries was carried to such fantastic extremes that the whole process of contract building became unwieldy, and the cost of building prohibitive.

On the other hand, land and houses were gradually becoming the property of banks, insurance companies, farm implement manufacturers, and real estate speculators. Inevitably the financial interests of these parasitic bodies ran counter to the needs of the families who used the property. The cause of the family went undefended. The real estate interests misrepresented the problem, since for them houses were commodities, not places to be lived in. It was to the advantage of the chain stores to have consumer groups centralized. The interest of the family was subordinated to the higher (and cleverly manipulated) law of supply and demand.

All along the line we see a disregard for those truths that flow from the mystery of the Incarnation. It has been forgotten that the family is a garden of souls. The home is the workshop of God. Under each roof a father and mother cooperate in the blessed work of creation. The politician has lost his sense of kingship. He has forgotten the dignity of the family as well as the dignity of his own high position. The carpenter and builder who shares his craft with Christ has placed wages before service as the end of his work. The unity of the Incarnation has been ignored, and consequently the integrity of man and of society has been lost.

IN CONCLUSION

I have briefly discussed four problems apparently unrelated, yet the solution to each proceeds from a true evaluation of the mystery of God become Man. Our error has been to classify all this as a *religious* view, something distinct from the economic view, the historical view or the practical view. Unconsciously, we have disincarnated God from the affairs of man. We dare to imply that God's ideas as to the disposition of His universe are of questionable practicality! That doubt explains our failure to relate Christian doctrine to the public practice. That is why Catholics constantly retreat to the borderline of that *which is sinful*, supposing that the Faith is only operative in the sphere of mortality. Most Catholics know that birth control is sinful. How many of them know what a beautiful thing sex is? And how very much more beautiful it is because of what has been added to marriage by the Incarnation of Christ! Christ is not merely a moralist; He is God. Christianity is not merely a way of avoiding sin; it is a way of living. The Church, who speaks for Christ, is not interested in *practical* matters as a side line to saving souls. Practical matters are the way that people save their souls. Lawyers do not save their souls as a result of the way they pray, but as a result of the way they practice law. A Christian lawyer can become a glorious lawyer or even a canonized lawyer like Saint Thomas More. If it is practical to separate spirit from matter, then the only practical man is the corpse.

The Faith reveals to us that God is always present in every movement of every creature in the universe. Of all His creatures, only man can disrupt the right order of the universe, and he can disorder the universe because he alone has the ability to choose.

Christ came to restore order to the universe. He became man to dispose the wills of men to the Will of His Father, for the wills of men were the seat of all the disorder in the universe. When He came the angels sang, "Peace on earth to men of good will," i.e., the restoration of order by disposing men's wills to the Will of God.

As Christ becomes one of us, we are given the awful privilege of becoming one with Him. Just as He shares our humanity, we consequently may share His divinity. The sharing of that divinity is called supernatural grace. Supernatural grace is the quality of soul which disposes our wills to the Will of God. Thus, as a result of the Incarnation, we have been given the proper disposition of will to reorder the whole universe. Our cooperation with God has not merely the force and efficacy of eager creatures, but, due to the grace of the Incarnation, it can have the potency and certainty of success which characterizes divine acts.

INTEGRITY: December, 1946

All the disorder around us will be resolved by the activity of the Christ-man, through the instrumentality of His members. That is our vocation and we are stuck with it. The cross is on our foreheads, not because we are worthy, not because we are saints, but because a babe was born of a Jewish virgin, and His name is Emmanuel — which means God with us.

ED WILLOCK
Boston
November 1946

There was a fond parent named Reedy
    Whose children were frightfully greedy,
Each Christmas he gave them
Something more to enslave them,
    While prayers he said for the needy.

The Church Year Consecrating the March of Time[*]

THE TITLE OF THIS ARTICLE, ON FIRST notice, seems to be a contradiction. What possible connection is there between the ecclesiastical year which slowly turns on its axis, presenting the same events year after year, and the "march of time" which rushes on at a faster pace each day, always presenting new ideas and new problems? Yes, these two concepts are opposed to each other, but they are not independent of each other.

They are opposed in the same sense that Creator is opposed to creature and eternity to time. But opposition does not exclude relationship. God certainly influences His creatures. Eternal truths definitely have a bearing on the passing things of time, and the re-enactment of the Life of Christ through the medium of the liturgical year certainly should have a bearing on our lives in the post war period (or any other period for that matter). Our ultimate goal is union with Christ in Heaven. Our immediate goal must be union with Christ on earth. The former cannot be obtained without the latter, and the closer the union is here, the closer it will be hereafter.

Obviously, the reason the liturgical year does not exert a greater influence upon our people is that they do not understand it. To most Catholics, it is simply another calendar, an ecclesiastical method of reckoning time and regulating religious holy days, a series of memorial services held to

---

[*] Reprint from *National Liturgical Week*, 1945. Peotone, Illinois: The Liturgical Conference Inc.

commemorate events in the Life of Christ and the saints. Considered merely in this light, the liturgical year would have little bearing on our present day life or on the events to come. However, it was never meant to be a mere recalling of things past. Our Lord came into the world for all of us. Everything He did, everything He said, was meant for us living in the twentieth century just as much as for those in the first. He is "the same yesterday and forever." (Heb. xiii, 8.) "Behold I am with you all days even unto the consummation of the world" (Matt. xxviii, 20.)

Sacramentally, He remains with us in the Holy Eucharist. Liturgically, He is longed for during Advent, born on Christmas, dies on Good Friday, returns to Heaven on Ascension Thursday and lives and operates through the Church during the Pentecostal season. The Church would have us regard these events not as fond memories of the past but as vital realities of the present.

Take for example the season of Advent. To most of our people, it means very little. They all know that it is a period of preparation for Christmas, but how to prepare is very vague in their minds.

Why it is a penitential season is a mystery to them. The trouble arises from a faulty and incomplete appreciation of the Feast of Christmas. We must not regard the birth of Christ just as a beautiful, momentous event of the past. Each year, on December 25, He is born for us again. He comes to save you and me and the lady next door and the man in the death house at the penitentiary. All of us have sinned and Christ comes to set us free. The great mystery of God becoming man is not a thing of the dim, distant past, but a vital, ever present reality, something that reaches back to the creation of man and extends forward to the end of the world.

The Incarnation is so great a mystery that the Church sets several weeks aside every year for its consideration. During Advent, we relive those thousands of years of watching, waiting, yearning. "Drop down dew, ye heavens from above and let the clouds rain the Just One; let the earth be opened and bud forth a Saviour." (Isa. xlv, 8.) In all truth we can sing this plea with the patriarchs of old, for we too are desperately in need of a Saviour. Our sins are great and numerous, but God's love is boundless. He is coming to save us. He wants to save us, if we will only let Him.

The consciousness of our sins, and, therefore, of our unworthiness of salvation, naturally moves us to works of penance. Hence the penitential character of Advent. It is unfortunately true that this aspect of the season is practically ignored nowadays. However, the mind of the Church is quite clear from the color of the vestments, the suppression of the *Gloria*, and other indications. Self denial is not very popular in these times, not even among Catholics, whether clerical or lay. Nevertheless the Church still desires it during Advent.

Very wisely, she opens the season with the picture of that other Coming of our Lord, when, in all power and majesty, He will judge the living and the dead. Our people wonder at these opening chords of the great Advent symphony. Why should it begin with the harsh notes of fear, when already the joyful melodies of the Christmas carols are ringing in our ears? Why should the awesome, the all-powerful, the just God be thrust upon us, when our thoughts naturally turn to the sweet babe of Bethlehem? Why? Because, although the Infant Jesus was born to save all men, all will not be saved. He cannot redeem me unless I am willing to be redeemed. If I do not prepare now for His coming as Saviour, I must be prepared to face Him later as Judge.

And so the Advent season opens with a call to penance, but lest we become too frightened and discouraged over our sins, the Church quickly reminds us that the final coming of Christ has not arrived. There is still time to avert the terror of the Last Day. The earth is about to bud forth a Saviour, and He that will arise shall rule the Gentiles and in Him shall the Gentiles have hope. The Epistle of the Second Sunday of Advent has the comforting words: "Now may the God of hope fill you with all joy and peace in believing; that you may abound in hope and in the power of the Holy Spirit." The same Saviour, yearned for so long throughout the Old Testament, is about to be born again. He is coming this Christmas for the same purpose He came nineteen hundred years ago — to save us.

As we get closer to His birth, the theme merges from one of hope into one of joy. The *Introit* of Gaudete Sunday introduces this third movement. "Rejoice in the Lord always, again I say, Rejoice." The Saviour is no longer Someone to come in the dim, distant future. He is already upon us. The *Invitatory* of Matins is no longer *"Regem venturum, Dominum,"* the Lord our coming King, but, *"Prope est iam Dominus, venite adoremus,"* the Lord is nigh, come let us adore Him. Fear is gone, hope is no longer needed; only joy fills our hearts now, in the anticipated possession of Christ our Infant Saviour.

The beauty of these first few weeks, like the remainder of the Church year, is unknown and unappreciated by most of our people. In preparing this paper I was interrupted many times by callers at the rectory. When I explained what I was doing, invariably they would ask the meaning of the title. Most of them thought it had something to do with Church history. After all, we cannot expect our congregation to know anything of the liturgical year when all we give it is passing mention in the announcements: "Today is the fourth

Sunday after the Epiphany. On Monday evening there will be bingo in the parish hall."

To make the liturgical year a source of grace in the march of time. We must keep up with the times. In former days, when life was simpler and distractions few, religion played a much more important part in the lives of the faithful. It was the center of all social activity. Nowadays, with the movies, radio, and automobile, the time set aside for church has been relegated to its minimum requirements. The personality of Christ, however, has an everlasting appeal; and it will overcome all obstacles if properly presented. We must use every possible device to keep the life of our Saviour ever present in the minds and hearts of our people.

The ceremonies prescribed for the feasts and various seasons of the year should be carried out with all possible solemnity, and should be clearly explained at the same time. The latter is most important, for unless a person sees and hears at the same time, his understanding can hardly be complete. Thus too, hymns appropriate to the time of the year should be sung instead of hackneyed numbers like *Mother Dear, O Pray for Me* and *To Jesus Heart all Burning*. Highlights of the liturgy for each week could be explained in the parish bulletin. Posters similar to those displayed at the various Liturgical Weeks and those printed by the Benedictine Fathers at St. John's Abbey (Collegeville, Minn.), can be effectively displayed in church and school. Many other suggestions to make people conscious of the ecclesiastical year may be found in the *Proceedings* of the previous Liturgical Weeks and in the magazine *Orate Fratres*.

Men are naturally influenced by their associates. Unconsciously, we are always taking on habits of dress, of speech, of thought, even physical mannerisms, from others. The liturgical year brings Christ down to earth and makes Him our constant Companion. Through the liturgy, we *see* Him in the various phases of His existence. He becomes a part of our lives, and we of His.

As time marches on faster each day, we cannot tell what the future will bring. We do know that a lasting peace must be founded upon a spiritual basis. Leaders in Church and State, in the army and navy, in journalism and commerce, have all told us this time and time again. The world is growing smaller day by day. The airplane and the radio, to mention but two factors, have drawn the nations of the earth much closer together, for better or for worse. The spiritual basis for unity and peace for Catholics is their common membership in the Mystical Body. But Christ is the Head of that Body and the Head must control the members.

Through the Church year, Christ assumes this leadership. He becomes a living reality, giving us His example, inspiring us to higher ideals. He speaks to us through the teaching of the Church, but He *shows* us through the liturgy. The former reaches only the intellect, the latter touches the heart. Through the proper celebration of the year, the life of Christ unfolds itself bit by bit, drawing us ever closer to Himself. He ceases to be a great Figure of the past, and emerges as the Light of the world now, today, and for all days to come.

JULES A. KEATING
Anniston, Alabama

BOOK REVIEWS

Belloc Revisited

THE SERVILLE STATE
By Hilaire Belloc.
New York: Henry Holt. 1946.
Price: $2.50.

Rereading this book (I read it about nine years ago — had I been born, I might have read it thirty-four years ago), these things struck me:

1) How long we have tolerated an economy which is radically wrong!

2) How long a few men (like Belloc) have been telling us how bad it is!

3) How long so many people have continued to believe in it in spite of men like Belloc and books like this one!

4) How very right Belloc was; how much more obviously right he is!

The positive statements of Mr. Belloc are inspiring to read. He drives his nails with long, sure strokes. Augustine could not have spoken thus against the Manichee. Dominic could not have preached so ruthlessly against the Albigensians. Augustine had been a Manichee before becoming a Christian. Saint Dominic might have felt that there were sincere Albigensians even though he knew that they were sincerely wrong. But those who could defend the philosophy (or lack of it) which tolerates capitalism are not deserving of the same respect.

Capitalism has always been through the belly, and with the belly, and of the belly, unto the Almighty Dollar, deceit without end. Amen. Its sin is beneath the theologian, beneath common sense, beneath common decency.

In this book we can see that a defense of the Faith can be at one and the same time a defense of the free family and of the man master of himself in his own home. We are reminded that only a philosophy can produce political action and a philosophy is only vital when it is the core of a religion.

Question: Are there young spirits who will continue the fight where this aged man must leave off? Is the servile state a portent for the future or is the current indifference an indication that it is already upon us?

ED WILLOCK

Conversion at Harvard

A TESTIMONIAL TO GRACE
By Avery Dulles.
New York: Sheed & Ward. 1946.
Price: $2.50.

Preoccupation with problems metaphysical and religious is not a characteristic which distinguishes contemporary American youth. With God's grace, there are a few exceptions. Avery Dulles is one of them. Catapulted to the brink of despair by the amoral, relativistic, positivistic society in which he found himself, he finally took refuge in Plato and Aristotle as a Harvard sophomore after a series of escapades in his freshman year (following logically in the wake of his own lack of principles) which all but culminated in his expulsion. His narrow escape had the sobering effect which was prelude to more serious application — and that, providentially, to the study of Aristotle and Plato, the following year. After discovery of objective standards of beauty and morality and truth through these giants, he came under the spell of a history tutor, Paul Doolin, an ardent young Catholic. Definitely turned to God, he wandered in pursuit of Him from one Protestant sect to another, his ancestors having been Presbyterians for generations. Aesthetically repelled by "Romanism" from the start, Avery Dulles' conversion was strictly one of thought (grace presupposed), not feeling. His conclusions were reached only after an extraordinarily searching examination of the Church's premises, historical and theological.

This is, thank God, not the subjective account of his gropings toward the Faith but a straightforward, concise resume of his ascent from truth to Truth, not more than a half hour's reading. In the main, it is closely reasoned argument at a high philosophical level well-sustained, and written with uncommon clarity and beauty of expression.

S.T

Miscellaneous Food For Thought

A CENTURY OF THE CATHOLIC ESSAY
Edited by Raphael H. Gross, C.PP.S.
Philadelphia: J. P. Lippincott Company, 1946.
Price: $3.50.

This book contains the cream of the cream of Catholic essays, culled from many years of discriminating reading on the part of the author. There is Mr. Sheed's magnificent piece on "Reading and Education." There is Christopher Dawson's "Christian Freedom," in which cosmic issues are explained lucidly, at a level a thousand times more profound than ordinarily. There is Msgr. Fulton J. Sheen at his very best, in "The Conspiracy Against Life." There is

Hilaire Belloc, "On Lying,"; Chesterton, both fascetious and scholarly, and Ronald Knox, and Father Gillis, and Padriac Colum, and Eric Gill and Alfred Noyes, and so on; forty-five essays in all. Congratulations to Father Gross and his publishers.

CAROL JACKSON

Potatoes For Christmas

MEDITATIONS WITH A PENCIL
By Diana Orpen.
New York: Sheed & Ward, 1946.
Price: $2.00.

Potatoes would be an unconventional Christmas gift. Only under certain circumstances would they be appreciated. A starving man would be grateful for them. He would be grateful if he were starving as a result of eating nothing but lemon meringue pie. This book of drawings is potatoes for people starving as a result of eating nothing but lemon meringue pie.

The general contention is that an artist should draw nothing but peaches, puddings or plums. This is particularly true if his art is called "religious." This is the psychological consequence of associating religion with the sentimental wish that everything were or will be "peachy."

The imagination is that room in the house most lived in by the sensate, and we are a sensate people. It is in this room that we receive visitors. We pray there, eat there, and it is there we sit down and make our evaluations. This habit puts a bit of a strain upon the truly religious artist whether he be poet or painter. When a simple illustrator (like Miss Orpen) enters the room of our imagination trying humbly to introduce us to her subjective "Christ." She finds the premises already crowded with gesticulating thespians all claiming to be Christ. From among the group her host emerges and choosing one of the actors, leads him to the artist and says, "*That* cannot be Christ, for *this* is He!" Of course the artist recognizes this odd fellow's disguise. He is playing the part of a renaissance "Christ." Across the room is a pre-Raphaelite 'Christ." On a raised dais sits a newcomer. He is a six-color, *Saturday Evening Post* cover "Christ."

The artist is tempted to remark, "But, can't you see that these are all a bunch of phoneys?" He doesn't because he has said it before and it did not work. The artist withdraws taking his work with him. He is hurt. It's all very unpleasant. What can be the trouble?

A picture is a public thing and therefore a social thing. The job of the artist is to translate something which is personal into something which is social. Now, it is in this very translation from the private to the social that the modern manifestation of Christianity is found wanting. This sphere, the natural habitat of the artist is a virtual no-man's land. It is that great desert between doctrine and practice. It is the area between Sunday Mass and the week day mess. Christians rarely enter that area today without putting on their face or grooming their inhibitions. Thus when the translation is made by an artist simply and sincerely in black and white the results appear very strange to our uncertain eyes.

I have said that Miss Orpen is sincere and simple in her work. Those are qualities that should be admired. The simplest way to draw is with a pencil on paper. That is what she did. The simplest way to draw the interior of a house is to draw from one's memory, boldly without regard for detail, shadow or perspective. That is what she did. The simplest way to draw people is to make a man look like a man, and a woman like a woman, and a baby look like a baby. That is what she did. Anything over and above this simplicity of approach is ornamentation or, if ill chosen, affection.

Admitted in her drawings you do not find the same effervescence of line and color one finds in Coca-Cola ads. Our education via the colored ad has harmed us in more ways than one. Not only has our stomach suffered but also our heads. The insincerity of pictorial ads is not limited to the description of the product, nor to its glorification of gluttony, but there is another kind of insincerity which is related to the making of things, in particular the making of pictures.

Now, anyone even a novice if he has at anytime felt the feeling that accompanies the act of making, is aware of the reciprocity between the maker and the thing being made. It is not a question of bending the medium to our will. The nature of the medium prescribes the manner in which it is to be used. Stone is brittle, oil is fluid, clay is plastic, and wood splinters. Lacking respect for his medium, the commercial artist has learned to impose his idea on it. He erases, adds, subtracts, cuts or fills in, until the smiling beauty emerges. This is not a normal procedure. The preconceived notions of the artist should not be forcefully applied to his medium but rather there should be a wedding of the two, and the finished product come as fruit of the marriage. That is the right way to draw. To work that way is to be sincere. Miss Orpen works that way. Her pencil strokes are fresh and unspoiled by erasers. Her people are made of paper and pencil. In her work we have the happy combination of sincere art with sincere faith.

Miss Orpen has not drawn peaches. She has drawn potatoes with an awkward dignity, and just enough dirt on them to show their earthy origin. These pictures are the fruit of meditation. They could be the seed for meditation if you would let them.

F. MARTIN

More Burdens For The White Man

TALE OF THE TWAIN.
By Sam Constantino Jr.
New York: Harper & Bros., 1946.
Price: $2.50.

Sam Constantino, Jr. has written a very readable story in *Tale of the Twain*. As the title suggests, it is the age-old story of religious intolerance. Much has been said and written about the down-trodden Negroes of these democratic United States. Far too little has been presented to us of the difficult position of the Orientals who have settled here, particularly on our West Coast.

This is the story of Tanako, a beautiful Eurasian who loves and tries to fit in with both races only to be rejected by both. We see the effects of the war with Japan upon Tanako, her Japanese lover, Koyohito, Stuart Crane, the American who is greatly attracted to her, and their friends in both countries. Mr. Constantino reveals convincingly to what a great extent the Japanese were victims of militarist propaganda.

The publishers describe the author as "a practical-minded young Christian writer." To our mind the novel is not a Catholic one, nor a Christian one. The ideals of Thomas Crump, who apparently voices the author's sentiments, are high but very human. He pleads that the Japanese be forced to think "democratically" for their own good, and for the good of mankind, if we are to avoid future catastrophic warfare. Stuart Crane, Sr. speaks in behalf of equal rights for Japanese Americans, but his motives too are those of expediency. He does not wish his son's sons to fight a third war.

Perhaps the adjective "practical" comes as consequence of the author's clinging to a shallow humanism while waging a cross-less crusade. Had he suggested supernatural motives and supernatural means, no doubt the blurb would have read "an impractical-minded young Christian writer."

D.W

APPENDIX
Prospectus

IT'S TIME FOR . . .

INTEGRITY

A Monthly Review
of Today's Problem
in the Light of
Catholic Teaching.

WE TAKE PLEASURE IN PRESENTING THE HON. EDWARD McCLELLAN O'BRIEN, distinguished citizen, prominent banker, trustee of this, and honorary member of that. Until recently the Hon. Edward assumed as a matter of course that he reflected honor on the Church and virtue on himself by his steady rise through worldly means to the top of his worldly calling, especially in view of his unblemished domestic reputation and his conspicuous Catholic practice.

That was before his only daughter went to a psychoanalyst. That was before his oldest son left the Church, and his youngest son declined to go to law school. That was before his wife developed discontent and he started to hear unfavorable rumors about high banking circles....

HELPFUL HARRIET IS TRYING TO BE HOLY. She gives money to a beggar; he goes out and gets drunk. She sweetly acquiesces to working overtime whenever asked; and has a nervous breakdown. She minds her sister's children; so their parents can sit in fashionable bars. She does all the housework; while those who ought to help with it cultivate the capital vices of pride and sloth.

Harriet is beginning to suspect that the meek virtues alone are not an infallible guide to universal sanctity....

MEET YOUNG FATHER McFADDEN, CURATE AT ST. MARY OF THE ANGELS. Every time he starts a young people's society it turns out to be a provocation for gala social events at which Father McFadden is an overworked vigilante committee of one. On top of that, he has run into a nest of disgruntled parish veterans who more than hint that they aren't anxious to devote their lives to Amalgamated Teacup.

Father doesn't like to admit it, but he doesn't know the answers....

THIS IS BILLY THE BUM. He found banking dull; so he left it. He thought advertising immoral; so he resigned. The commercial stench of retailing made him nauseous; so he quit. Selling stocks and bonds repelled him from afar. One week in radio was enough.

Everybody feels sorry for Billy because *he doesn't fit in*. Billy has his own sorrow, that although he's a wonderful critic, he can't figure out a blueprint for a better order....

BEHOLD JENNIFER, THE BEST-DRESSED DAILY COMMUNICANT IN ST. STEPHEN'S PARISH. Fellow parishioners are all-admiring. Jennifer appears to have effected a neat reconciliation between God and Mammon. The magic formula:

worldly success + exceptional piety = the ideal Catholic girl

What has happened to those curious gospel admonitions about becoming a fool for Christ's sake and bringing down the hate of the world upon your head? . . .

SEAN KEVIN PATRICK MURPHY IS THE TOP CATHOLIC ACTION LEADER AT ST. MALACHY'S COLLEGE. He exudes personal magnetism. Freshmen worship his careless air of command. Seniors respect his initiative and zeal. Professors are delighted that one so richly endowed should seek his daily spiritual food at the seven o'clock Mass and publicly acknowledge his allegiance to the Almighty.

Sean has made it possible to say grace openly at the campus cooperative restaurant. Sean has persuaded fellow students to greet each other at random. Sean has reduced the heavy liquor consumption at fraternity dances.

But don't ask Sean what comprehensive plans he has for the Christian order of the future. He hasn't any. . . .

SISTER MARY ANGELA CHRISTOPHER TEACHES FRENCH AT MT. ARDUOUS. "Je vous salue, Marie..." chants the class, and then plunges into its mundane studies. The Sophomores are learning to send out their laundry from a French hotel they are unlikely ever to visit. The Seniors are translating expurgated versions of works which in their entirety would rate the Index.

Sister Mary Angela Christopher wants to teach her students about the love of God, but that isn't her subject and the students resent having it thrown in without credit. Once she had it in mind to use Catholic Action literature and St. Theresa's autobiography for classroom reading, but the scheme turned out to be incompatible with something called accreditation. . . .

ALL these people are our friends, lightly disguised. They are nice people. They want to lead Christian lives. Besides their good-will, they have this in common: they are a little vague as to what constitutes a Christian lay life today. No wonder, for that is **the** problem of the day. For them, and for all of us who are trying to live the faith, we are publishing.

INTEGRITY

WHAT IS INTEGRITY?

INTEGRITY is a monthly magazine.

IS IT CATHOLIC?

It is a lay magazine whose staff is Catholic. While not speaking *ex cathedra*, its editors see no hope for our society apart from the Church.

WHY DO YOU CALL IT INTEGRITY?

We call it INTEGRITY because we admire that quality and propose to cultivate it. We call it INTEGRITY to suggest a re-integration of religion and life in the modern world. This is *the* central problem which the magazine will consider.

IS IT A SERIOUS MAGAZINE?

Very.

WILL IT BE DULL?

Never.

WILL IT HAVE PICTURES?

Cartoons, Jingles too.

WHAT WILL IT BE ABOUT?

It will be about the problems of Catholic lay life: such problems as family life, psychiatry, women in contemporary society, education, the land movement, the movies, security and God's Providence, trends in medicine, inter-racial considerations, organic farming, work, and the radio.

Each issue will center around one particular subject. The basic problems in connection with that subject will be discussed. The basic problems on any subject have moral and religious considerations. In this sense, in that we shall not treat of superficialities, INTEGRITY will be a radical magazine.

CAN YOU GIVE AN EXAMPLE OF WHAT AN ISSUE WILL BE LIKE?

Yes. The November issue will treat of the lay apostolate. There will be a survey of lay apostolic activities in the United States. There will be a report on post-war Catholic Action in Europe. There will be an article on the Catholic Worker movement, another on The Grail. There will be a discussion of the theology back of Catholic Action.

Another example. In February we shall treat of contemporary Protestantism. There will be pictures and pen portraits of Bishop Oxnam, Reinhold Niebuhr and some of the other outstanding Protestant figures. There will be articles on the movement toward Rome within the Protestant churches, on the efforts toward Protestant unity, on Communist-Protestant affiliations. There will be a discussion of intercredal cooperation, and a glimpse into the way ordinary Protestants feel about the Roman Catholic Church.

HOW MUCH WILL INTEGRITY COST?

25 cents an issue, $3.00 a year (12 issues).

WHO WILL BE THE WRITERS?

The vital Catholic thinkers of the day. Those who have managed to see the problems of their particular professions or communities in the light of Catholic teaching. Some are already well-known; most are the Chestertons, Bellocs, Eric Gills and Peter Maurins of the era now dawning.

WHEN WILL THE FIRST ISSUE APPEAR?

October 1, 1946.

Address: 1556 York Avenue, New York 28, New York

Associates: John Murphy and Doreen O'Sullivan

Editors: Edward Willock and Carol Jackson

INTEGRITY will devote itself to spreading abroad the truth. We hold with Peguy that he who does not bellow the truth when he knows the truth makes himself the accomplice of liars and forgers. We are not interested in academic truths about the population of Madagascar in 1856, or the authenticity of a Browning signature. Only a stable, well-ordered society has the leisure to speculate on such non-essentials. Our times are critical. We shall publish, therefore, vital truth about vital problems of the day.

We shall not cater to our reading public in the sense of exploiting their sentiments in order better to line our own pockets. The fruits of such a policy, all too evident around us, are the degradation of public intelligence and taste. Since Adam's time, and the loss of original integrity, we have always been vulnerable to appeals made to our lower natures.

Neither shall we assume literary airs and thus restrict ourselves to an academic elite. We value culture not at all as compared to holiness. We shall present our ideas as clearly, forcibly, and as interestingly as we possibly can. It is difficult enough to understand our confused times without our placing any unnecessary obstacles in the way.

If our magazine is also entertaining, it is not because we think the public is in need of any more recreation. It is partly because being engaged in a Christian endeavor which is very much to our taste makes us light-hearted, and partly because the only way to deal with the ridiculous is to laugh at it.

St. Thomas More is our patron saint. He stood firm in a world of slippery consciences and specious reasoning. He lost his head only once, and then in a good cause.

That we may preserve our integrity in times as difficult,

ST. THOMAS MORE   PRAY FOR US

Also available from
AROUCA PRESS

Meditations for Each Day
Antonio Cardinal Bacci (pbk & hb)

Fraternal Charity
Fr. Benoît Valuy, S.J.

The Epistle of Christ:
Short Sermons for the Sundays of the Year
on Texts from the Epistles
Fr. Michael Andrew Chapman

Our Lady, A Presentation for Beginners
Dom Hubert van Zeller, O.S.B.

www.ingramcontent.com/pod-product-compliance
Lightning Source LLC
Chambersburg PA
CBHW060352080526
44583CB00012B/275